To

_____

From

_____

ONE DAE AT A TIME

Keepers International Publishing
Copyright 2020
ISBN: 978-0-9983208-8-5

www.keepersinternational.org/publishing

Table of Contents

Table of Contents

A NOTE FROM THE FOUNDER

WELCOME, MY BEAUTIFUL FRIENDS.

I'm so excited that you are taking this journey with us. As Intentional Women it's so important that we take the time to invest in ourselves. This devotional was created for you. I am humbled as the Founder of Intentional Women for having the faith to trust God and the foresight to embrace this journey.

For a FB tribe like Intentional Women, there is no more fitting time for our tribe. I am honored to be entrusted with a group of women that has broken so much ground in its first year of existence. Intentional Women is a group that doesn't just post for fun on Facebook; it stands for something. We embrace the idea that women living intentionally serve a purpose in our world that goes beyond just a fancy slogan, and that responsible and consistent actions can be a vehicle for progress.

We believe these higher goals don't contradict the quest for breakthrough in our lives. On the contrary, we're convinced women that reflect and embody these values will be tomorrow's leaders. We are passionately interested in the nitty-gritty of what makes women work well together and celebrate the creative people in all types of industries, at all levels, who inspire innovation.

As you will soon see, this book is full of Declarations, Affirmations and Encouragement. The title came from thinking of my great Auntie and her beautiful life that she lived before she recently transitioned. What she would tell everyday is to "take it one day at a time". That is exactly what we need to do in our everyday lives.

To get the most out of this book you must be all in! Take notes, journal, share your experiences and make the commitment to be INTENTIONAL.

If you know someone that should join our tribe, share the information with them. Email info@kimberlysolomon.org or visit www.officialintentionalwomen.com

Kimberly M. Solomon

Kimberly M. Solomon
Founder of Intentional Women

IW
INTENTIONAL
WOMEN

AFFIRMATIONS

Positive affirmations
are very
powerful because
they release you from
negativity, fear, worry,
and anxiety. When
these affirmations are
repeated over and
over again, they begin
to take charge of your
thoughts, slowly
changing your
pattern of thinking
and ultimately
changing your life.

FOREWORD

Cheryl Polote-Williamson

Award-Winning,
Multi-Best-Selling Author
and Transformational Speaker
Entrepreneur, Philanthropist,
and Women's Advocate
CEO & Founder of Soul
Reborn, Inc.

www.cherylpwilliamson.com

FOREWORD

I believe in WORD POWER. Very simply put, I believe you have what you say. I believe that God has given us the power to create with words—to shape our environments, our lives, our future with words. Moreover, I believe in the affirming Word of God. I am a living example of having the guts to say about myself, what God says about me—to feel about myself what God feels about me, and the audacity to believe it all. Everything that I am; every book I've written; every opportunity granted; every award, title, or position I hold is because of the favor of God on my life and the words that I speak out of my mouth. It's how my husband and I live. There is something powerful about coming into agreement with the Word, then in daily affirmations, using the Word and positive thoughts to frame your world and call into being the desires God has placed in your heart. There is something equally satisfying about running into someone with the same belief system and practices.

Three years ago, when Kimberly and I met at a conference in Florida, there was an instant connection. It wasn't long before I discovered that she and her husband both are also on fire for God, pour the Word of God into their children, and that they live by the power of affirmations. Since that time, both our sisterly bond and spiritual connection have grown. Not only do we share a love for the empowerment and advancement of women and helping them intentionally live out their purpose on purpose; but also Kimberly became a part of my Affirmed community and co-author in my anthology—Soul Source: 23 Soulful Stories of Women Who Relied on God During Difficult Times. Her husband, Keith, joined my team of co-authors in Soulful Prayers: The Power of Intentional Communication with God. These are just a few of the ways we've connected that speak to the reason I could not be more pleased to invite you to change your life, reshape your world, and grab hold of all you desire using One DAE at a Time!: Intentional Declarations, Affirmations, and Encouragement for Women as your guide. Kimberly Solomon has the heart of God and her finger on the pulse of what women need in order to thrive. Speaking the right things in and over our lives is a part of that. Kimberly has a giving spirit. She longs to support you and have you flourish.

Allow her and her chosen co-authors to guide you with this powerful and insightful collection of daily spoken Word and positive beliefs from One DAE at a Time!: Intentional Declarations, Affirmations, and Encouragement for Women. I know that my connection to Kimberly has been a blessing. Allow this same blessing to flow from her to you. Start today—declaring and affirming, and getting the encouragement you didn't even know you needed; and watch it change your world!

Cheryl P. Williamson

January

JANUARY 1

Goal Setting

Use today to set your goals for the year.
Be clear and specific with what you want to achieve.
Break the goal down into steps.
All the best in achieving your goals this year!

_____

_____

_____

_____

_____

_____

_____

_____

_____

_____

_____

_____

_____

_____

I am grateful and blessed to be in my current position

We will celebrate each other more than we criticize!

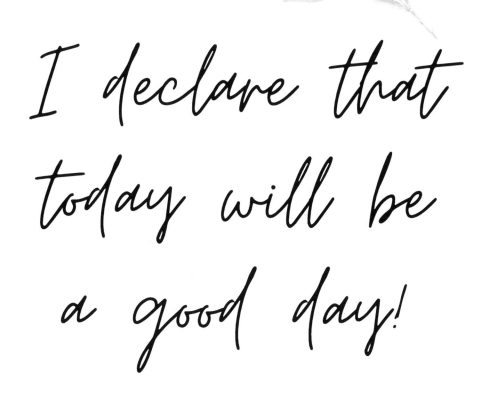

I declare that today will be a good day!

JANUARY 5

DECLARATION: I decree and declare that I am worthy, and I am enough.
AFFIRMATION: I am valuable even when I do not produce or perform.

A couple of years ago, I made a faith decision that changed the trajectory of my life. I went from being a sought-after professional in the workplace to unemployed. I went from being respected in my community to the unknown and unvetted. I started over practically from scratch; to sit and rest without my list of attributes, achievements, and accomplishments preceding me. As an undiagnosed high achiever, I did not realize just how much completed to-do lists meant to me. This new normal was strange and unsettling. Sound familiar? As women, we are taught to find worth in productivity and performance. We are the go-to person, the problem solver, and the one everyone can trust to execute with proficiency and excellence. If we are not careful, these achievements begin to define us, to our detriment.

Others reap the benefits, but we are left exhausted and depleted. If we only find value handling business, our ears become dull to God's voice, and the distance grows from His presence. We identify our value through productivity and performance alone. Hence, we get sidelined, the discomfort is unbearable, and we believe that we no longer have worth. God values us not because of what we do, but simply because we are His. A relationship is invaluable to God so much that He gave his life to foster one with us.

Relationships develop with intimacy. Intimacy requires time. It is not just time using our talents to perform and produce, but also the time in prayer, time studying the Word of God, time worship or contemplative reflection, and time listening to His instruction. We should prioritize God's presence over performance. God wants us surrendered, leaning in, and seeking Him as our source, not always grinding or glorifying ourselves as the resource. This is a clarion call to redefine worth. Sit at His feet, basking in His presence, soak in His wisdom, and be restored.

Today, I implore you, stop performing long enough to get instructions from the director and writer of your life's script. If He takes your storyline in another direction, trust the almighty, powerful one who knows your end from your beginning to orchestrate things behind the scenes for your good and His glory. Welcome His presence into the green room of your hearts, the secluded places with minimal access. He wants to remind you that you
are His and that alone is enough!

Charla Armstead

JANUARY 6

I declare that I am able to handle anything that comes my way

I declare positivity to rain over me today!

<u>JANUARY 8</u>

I am confident
and capable

JANUARY 9

Enter His gates with thanksgiving and His courts with praise; give thanks to him and praise His name. For the Lord is good and His love endures forever; His faithfulness continues through all generations.
Psalms 100:4-5

I am confident
and capable

JANUARY 11

Praise the Lord.

Give thanks to the Lord, for He is good; His love endures forever.

Psalms 106:1

I decree and declare that all negative thoughts are gone

I declare positivity to rain over me today!

JANUARY 14

Prayer List

Take the time to pray for others today and put their names below

_____
_____
_____
_____
_____
_____
_____
_____
_____
_____
_____
_____
_____
_____
_____

JANUARY 15

DECLARATION: I decree and declare that the power of God soothes my soul and energizes my spirit!

AFFIRMATION: I am able to release the pain and heal, when I put my faith into action, and walk in God's Glory!

On November 16, 2018, the house phone rang at 5:00 a.m. I did not answer it. Immediately after the cell phone rang, I answered it reluctantly. On the other end was a detective and he confirmed that I was my brother's sister. He informed me that my brother was hit by a train, I said, "What precinct do I go to?" and he said, "No"! Yelling at him I said, "What hospital is he in?" The detective said, "No hospital, he was killed!" I began to scream, cry, and jump up and down. I could barely breathe. I think I remember the detective attempting to calm me down as he went on with the details. I became numb and immobilized. I screamed! The detective requested that I call someone while he was on the phone. I questioned the detective, "Are you sure"?
I called my daughter, his daughter, relatives, and friends. I called the detective back because it seemed like a dream. I began to pray. I asked God to please come and comfort me. I called my Pastor I needed Prayer. I went through the motions of meeting with family, viewing his body and meeting with the detectives. Reality did not exist.

I lost the only sibling left, my baby brother. Emotions were running through my heart; I lost a piece of me; no more morning calls no more requesting money, no more Thanksgiving and Christmas dinners or him sitting at the head of the table and reminding me that he is a Great Chef. I asked God to please rescue me from this pain. I prayed so hard and long that I knew everything depended on God in order for me to be able to continue. Thank goodness for my Church family. God put the most caring people in my life when I needed them the most. This loss was like a bad dream. I wanted to run away. My mind was telling me I had to be strong for my brother's daughter. I felt at that time; only God could make a way. I seemed to carry on in a sphere of almost non- existence. My mind could not rest; I was unable to sleep. I was continually praying and asking God for his mercy and grace. I know my brother's physical being is gone, but his memory continues to live. I feel his presence every day when I hear the birds sing and when I see his daughter and grandchildren.

Death does not stop one's existence or their memories from flowing. I reflect on God's goodness in the past, and I know He will see me through. I am still standing in God's glory! God can awaken our faith to be more durable and to use our gifts to love and comfort others experiencing loss. We can conquer all pain when we walk in God's presence! We must trust God and have faith in his love for us. We must serve others, and as we serve others, we serve God and heal ourselves!

Robbin Johnson

Come, let us sing for joy to the Lord; let us shout aloud to the Rock of our salvation. Let us come before him with thanksgiving and extol him with music and song. For the Lord is the great God, the great King above all gods.

Psalms 95:1-3

I am in charge of my thoughts

JANUARY 18

DECLARATION: I decree and declare that forgiveness is not for the person who hurt me, it's for me.

AFFIRMATION: I am a child of God who is proud of her heritage and I come from a strong line of women!

Encouragement? How do you define it? How do you measure it? How do you embody it? How do you become an encouragement for someone else? I confess I didn't struggle with these questions because I was blessed to have the perfect personification of encouragement in my life – my mother. But not just my mother, it also was the long lineage of strong, independent, entrepreneurial, God-focused, and loving Black Women from which I come who were, and remain, my encouragement foundation. The answers seemed pretty straightforward, or so I thought until I began to dig deeper into what made them and subsequently me.

It happened when my mother was diagnosed with dementia and needed medical care and daily living support. She didn't want to go to a nursing home, and she didn't want to leave her husband, my stepfather, alone. After much deliberation with my siblings, my husband and I proposed moving her from St. Thomas to live with us in our home in Maryland. My mother made it abundantly clear she only would move if we welcomed her husband as well. Never in my wildest dreams did I imagine that in my "golden years," I would have to confront the unspoken trauma and pain of my childhood, and forgive and care for the person responsible, my stepfather.

It was at this moment I realized two things: one, my love for my mother outweighed the pain from my childhood abuse, and two, the only way I would or could forgive was to get closer to God. Only He would take the pain away, fill my heart with love and teach me to be a blessing. If I would trust and follow Him, He would lead me through. You see, I thought I had forgiven my stepfather years ago, but providing for him the same way and in the same capacity I provided for my mother was more than challenging. It was agonizing until I saw and began to understand my Mother's Love for my stepfather. It was the same unconditional love she had for and showed to me, and her family, her friends, her God. It was what made her a Blessing. It was what taught me encouragement!

I learned during that season; I needed to forgive my stepfather not for him but myself. I learned I was blocking my blessings because of unforgiveness. Once I was able to forgive genuinely, a huge burden was lifted, and my purpose in that season was crystal clear. Forgiveness is for you, my friend. Make no mistake; if it weren't for prayer and a deeper relationship with God, I would not have made it. God placed love in my heart and gave me the strength to complete the task. Encouragement? To hear God say, "Well done, my good and faithful Servant."

Edith Chatman

JANUARY 19

DECLARATION: I decree and declare that through the bountiful arms of the LORD, I am the change in my life to make all things possible.

AFFIRMATION: I am the change.

Isn't it insane how this world can knock you down just when you think you have made it? As the old saying goes, "I cannot win for losing." Or have you been knocked down so often it is becoming routine? I started to see a monumental shift in my life when I changed my way of thinking. I came upon the realization that it was me that held power. I held power to make the change. I had to be the change to become the best version of me.

Several turning points took place in my life before I started to see a shift in my foundation towards a better version of me. I had to release certain obligations and debts, I believed were holding me back from progressing. Just because I felt something was owed to me did not make it so. Fuel and motivation are what I took from my "No."

However, what was unique about me was my inner will, my desire, and drive to make the change in myself that I wanted to see. The metamorphosis of becoming the best version of you starts with YOU. So,are you ready for a supernatural change? Are you ready for a change that will restructure what once held you down?

Are you ready for a change that will exponentially expand your mind? We owe it to ourselves to carve out a fantastic path that will lead us to exactly where we truly want to be. All while withstanding the bumps that will come along the way. So, first things first, get focused! It all starts with a bright, vivid, vibrant thought and will grow into something superabundant if executed with a focused purpose. A focused plan leads to a focused journey, and a focused journey will lead to the change in you. Think, walk, talk, and act with focus!

Here are seven life-affirming statements to take with you on your focused journey. Repeat them often and become the change you want to see!

I will focus my thoughts and not become distracted.
I will focus my energy and not become drained.
I will focus on strengthening my abilities and not become defeated.
I will focus on improving my skills and not let not knowing, hold me back.
I will focus on completing my goals and not dwell in procrastination.
I will focus on looking upward and onward and not letting the past determine my future.

I am the change. It starts with me.

Windi Floyd-Reynolds

I do not judge
myself
unrighteously

JANUARY 21

Prayer List

Take the time to pray for others today and put their names below

I am in charge of my thoughts

JANUARY 23

DECLARATION: I decree and declare that I am no longer in the bondage of darkness, and I walk in the freedom light of the Lord.

AFFIRMATION: I am a woman of God that fully trusts is in the Lord because He is the only answer to prayer.

I grew up in the South Bronx projects, living in a household of eight siblings with me nine (two girls and seven boys). On January 23, 1973, it was my first episode of using alcohol and drugs. It was my 13th birthday party, which I felt privileged stepping into the teenage world. We had soul food, liquor, beer, cigarettes, and marijuana (reefer), just like the grown-ups I witnessed, particularly my mother. Little did I know I was cosigning the beginning of my experimental drugging days.

My party reminded me of the "Cooley High" (produced by Spike Lee) movie drinking a lot of Old English 800 beer and getting drunk. Smoking my first cigarette/reefer and dancing with a boy in the corner, hoping not to get caught by my brothers or mother. Someone started a fight, and we had to throw the troublemaker out. Labeled a smart dummy, I thought I could take one puff and get away with it. After the party and being exposed to beginner drugs, I acquired a street name, Queen of Cheeba. Cheeba was another name for marijuana.

My drug use continued into adulthood with a hallucinating drug in the '70s, which escalated to Cocaine, freebase, and later called crack in the 1980s. In the height of my crack days, I knew I needed emergency help, a miracle worker to save me from the miserable life of crack. While using one night, I got on my knees and begged God to deliver me, and He heard my cry and pulled me out of the pit of darkness and into His marvelous light! That's when I knew He answers a sinners' prayer.

Through the finished works of Jesus Christ, we have been redeemed and delivered from sin to freedom from the captivity of drug addiction. God sent two of His servant daughters to do His bidding and work a miracle through them by teaching me how to study the bible to develop a personal relationship with Him. Our Heavenly Father keeps watching over the sinners and the righteous ones. In the middle of our troubles, we must confidently stand on God's promises because He loves and cares for us. When we seek Him, we will find Him.

God loved us first, and He's a good gracious Father who works for our good and His purpose. He covers over a multitude of sins and forgives us for our mistakes. He's only one who answers prayers. We can always trust that the Lord knows best for each of His children.

Althea Belton

JANUARY 24

DECLARATION: I decree and declare that my flaws are not imperfections but battle wounds that cast out the perfect shade of His beauty as He alone has kept me.

AFFIRMATION: I am unique, there are no other designs like me for I am an original intense warrior, a builder, and a birther.

Like many, perhaps life has given you a different meaning to what beauty is. In today's society, beauty has many degrees. It can be characterized by a model's body or smashingly fine captivating and all featured woman. It can be defined by money as fascinating of the thought, tasty looking dish appealing on a plate or words spoken so profoundly that the only word to describe them is beautiful. It can also be defined by a personality that is so pleasing until it is described as stunning. During one period of my life, I struggled with my idea of beauty. I often identified beauty as things; material things.

If I didn't dress a certain way or have a certain thing, I didn't find myself beautiful. I too often looked for surface beauty because I hadn't searched the depths of myself for inner beauty. I would often find myself degrading others because I did not see myself as beautiful. As a young girl growing up, many obstacles made me doubt anything about me could be beautiful.

My idea of perfection was entangled in possessions. I was frequently told, "You are so beautiful. You are pretty." My mother made sure she spoke words of life into her children. She assured me regularly about these things. Yet, inside I felt ugly. I thought that I didn't meet the standards of the world beauty. Why is it that others can sometimes see what we cannot? It was my mother's words that would assist in building my identity. It would be some of her words and discovering my identity in Christ that would help secure my idea of beauty. As I begin a journey of deliverance, I came to grips with my perceived inadequacy, and I started on a path of forgiving myself for self-hatred. When I forgave myself, my beauty began to shine brighter as I start to allow the light of Christ to shine through the broken places, a broken child of God, a beautiful child of God.

Forgiveness is essential to see your beauty. YOU ARE BEAUTIFUL!

Do you see yourself as beautiful? What is your idea of beauty? How does your concept of beauty impact your life? I am here to encourage you not to let your idea of beauty change your life but to allow God to show you how beautiful you are!

Chiquita Dallas

JANUARY 25

I will praise God's name
in song and glorify
him with thanksgiving.

Psalms 69:30

JANUARY 26

Encouragement

Take the time to encourage yourself today. Write down your wins for the month!

_____
_____
_____
_____
_____
_____
_____
_____
_____
_____
_____
_____
_____
_____
_____
_____

JANUARY 27

DECLARATION: I decree and declare that God will deliver me from whatever my life brings before me. I need only trust that He knows what is best for me.

AFFIRMATION: I am willing to trust God to not only deliver me from every storm but to use it for my edification and His glory.

Have you ever experienced something that totally uprooted your reality and shook you intensely at your core? Was it a painful divorce or a job opportunity you took that ended up being a bad decision? Were you betrayed by a close friend and family members? Was it one of your children lashing out excessively due to his/her internal struggles? Did you look in the mirror and saw someone you didn't recognize? If one or two of these incidents occurred, it would send most of us to the altar several Sundays in a row. Now, imagine dealing with all of these at the same time. Yes, each of these incidents occurred in my life within months, if not weeks, of each other. That would leave anyone feeling shattered into what felt like a million pieces, never feeling whole again. Admittedly, there were tears shed almost every day for close to three months straight. The proverbial "WHY ME LORD?"

He was undoubtedly a part of my daily outcry to God. In times like these, it is easy to relive our pain as a regular part of our daily routine. Playing out what went wrong over and over again in our minds. One day, as I was taking a walk, I decided not to listen to any music or sermons in my earbuds. I was intentionally desiring to talk to God. Before I knew it, I was deep in my "Lord, you know what I've been through" rant. My all to familiar, "I don't understand God! Why would You want me to endure so much pain" soliloquy? I immediately heard Him ask, "Rubye, what is your most prized possession?" I replied, "My children, of course." He said, "Well, how did they get here?" My mind began to recall my pregnancies, my time in the delivery room, and the indescribable pain of childbirth. Anyone who has experienced it (or has even heard about it) knows it is the most excruciating pain ever!

At that moment, God clarified my struggles so clearly for me. He reminded me if my most prized possessions were born through such intense pain, I need to understand that there is certainly a prize and greater purpose on the other end of this exposure of pain that I was experiencing. Those are shouting words right there! That day I discovered we must shift our frame of reference when we are forced to digest even the most debilitating heartbreak and disappointment. I encourage you to remember there will be glory after your excruciatingly painful experiences. And, like childbirth, minimal recollection of the pain will exist once we behold the beauty of what we have birthed.

Rubye Dunn

JANUARY 28

Prayer List

Take the time to pray for others today and put their names below

_____

_____

_____

_____

_____

_____

_____

_____

_____

_____

_____

_____

_____

_____

_____

_____

JANUARY 29

I will give thanks to the Lord because of his righteousness; I will sing the praises of the name of the Lord Most High.

Psalms 7:17

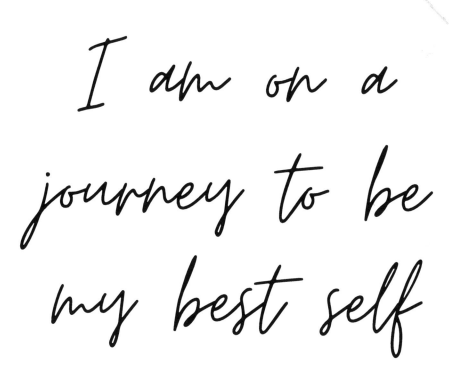

I am on a
journey to be
my best self

I am free to focus on my goals

February

FEBRUARY 1

Goal Setting

Use today to set your goals for the year.
Be clear and specific with what you want to achieve.
Break the goal down into steps.
All the best in achieving your goals this year!

_____

_____

_____

_____

_____

_____

_____

_____

_____

_____

_____

_____

_____

_____

_____

_____

FEBRUARY 2

DECLARATION: I decree and declare that I will never settle for less than what God has destined for my life because I will show up for myself even when it is hardest to do so.

AFFIRMATION: I am showing up powerfully in my own life, each day.

I was just 23 years old in the spring of 1999 when I found out I was pregnant with my son. I was living in a city without relatives, and my boyfriend told me, "if you have the baby, you will be doing it by yourself". My family was disappointed and shared their opinions about how I had ruined my life. I was quickly sat down from my leadership roles in the church and found myself alone and feeling helpless, and ashamed. Since that time, there have been countless hours when I felt inadequate. Days when I felt insecure about whom I had become—weeks when I was uncertain about my place in the world. More than anything, I felt guilty that I hadn't lived up to the life others had dreamt of for me.

When I couldn't find the motivation to push forward, my love for my son propelled me to do whatever needed to be done. I learned to move on autopilot and do all the things I felt I needed to do to be accepted. I had become a prisoner to my negative thinking about myself. I spent a great deal of time masking this from others, trying desperately to overachieve to gain their approval. So, I pushed hard (and still do) to be the best. I extended myself to others, sometimes beyond my capacity. I loved others even when I could not find reasons to love myself. Then, I found myself accomplished, on track with most of my life's goals, a leader in most places I existed, and entirely and undeniably miserable. I have faced some major disappointments in life and have made some bad decisions with long-lasting consequences. Having my son was not one of them. I punished myself for so long, and though I quickly extended forgiveness to others, I found myself incapable of offering that same grace to myself. At my breaking point, I felt as if I heard God merely saying, no more. In all the time I had spent trying to be great for others, I had settled in continual neglect of myself.

Mindset is one of the most powerful forces in a person's life, and conditioning your thinking for success takes a lot of time and effort. It started with a realization that I had positive control over myself, my life, and how I chose to process my experiences. If that was the case, I had both the power and responsibility to change my thinking in a lasting way. Life is hard, and the most natural human response to difficulty is to bow out and settle for less than we deserve. It is a journey, but when I finally decided to SHOW UP in my own life, the self-doubt and insecurity began to fade. We can be outstanding! It can be a work in progress, but we must decide to start showing up in our own lives, vowing to shift beyond our obstacles and living each day purposely in empowerment. We must no longer disrupt God's destiny for our lives and know that what we can achieve with God on our side is limitless. Then, we must be committed to helping others reach that same conclusion.

Chrissy Thornton

FEBRUARY 3

With praise and thanksgiving they sang to the Lord: "He is good; his love toward Israel endures forever." And all the people gave a great shout of praise to the Lord, because the foundation of the house of the Lord was laid.

Ezra 3:11

FEBRUARY 4

I am loved by God!

FEBRUARY 5

DECLARATION: I decree and declare that my family, my seed and my bloodline will fulfill the purpose that God has for us, and surrender our will and walk out the call of God on our lives.

AFFIRMATION: I am a woman God, I have given up my control and have allowed God to take total control of my life.

In 1991 something gave birth that changed the lives of my entire family. I went from living a loving family dream to who turned the lights out. There were times I didn't know what to say or how to feel. My emotions were all over the place—angry one minute, to being suicidal and helpless another. As I prayed and sought God, He revealed to me, if I would surrender, give up and let go of everything. He would take all of the pain, hurt, and heartache, and in return, He would give me strength, a life of purpose, a life of victory, and everlasting love.

If we want real change in our lives, if we want true peace and joy, which only comes from God...the world cannot give it; God requires us to surrender. God's will for our personal life is done through the emptying or dying of self, putting self aside. This ultimate surrender is obedience, and obedience to God brings about His will in our lives, resulting in lasting effects often associated with earthly and divine blessings. God was thinking about you and me before He created the earth. He chose us to be His children when time on earth would come. He knew about your human weaknesses long before you were born. The fact that God chose you is no coincidence; it was His will. Trust in the Lord entirely, do not rely on your own opinions; with all your heart rely on Him to guide you and lead you in every decision you have to make. When we become intimate (draw near) with the Lord in whatever circumstance we face in life, He will lead us in the right direction. Don't think for a moment that you know it all; wisdom comes when you adore Him with undivided devotion and avoid everything contrary to God's word.

There is no limit to what God can do with a person who is yielded and willing to do His will. God wants to bring you into a new, stronger covenant relationship with Him, in which you no longer depend upon the natural, limited resources of this world. You are filled with the Holy Spirit's overflowing power, and He wants to influence the world through you. This power will enable you to be strengthened to win every battle and be excellent in character. Man looks at the outward appearance, but God sees the beauty of the heart. With passion, answer God's call and keep yielding to Him as one who has now experienced the resurrected life! You live now for His pleasure, ready to be used for His purpose. Strip yourself of the old nature and allow your mind to be renewed and clothe yourself with God's virtue. His plans for your life will unfold right before you, and he will order your footsteps. Just trust Him. A life surrendered to God, overcomes every challenge.

Chanda Bacon

FEBRUARY 6

Do not be anxious about anything, but in every situation, by prayer and petition, with thanksgiving, present your requests to God. And the peace of God, which transcends all understanding, will guard your hearts and your minds in Christ Jesus.
Philippians 4:6-7

FEBRUARY 7

I radiate beauty and joy

FEBRUARY 8

I am a powerhouse

FEBRUARY 9

Have you ever wanted something so bad that you moved on through life, and later on you realized that delay is not denial? Well, that was me. I 've always had a desire to become a nurse. I remember the moment I got my acceptance letter in the mail. I was so excited that I wanted to share it with my friends and family. I remember informing my Commander at the time about the good news. She seemed to be more excited than I was; she began prepping my future based on the information I gave her. I was so determined that I was willing to travel to another state to attend school.

While attending school, I started carpooling with two other ladies who made my commute much more comfortable, and long-term friendships were created. With only having four classes left until I obtained my nursing degree, I missed my final by two points, which caused me to have to sit out for two years. I remember going to my car to be alone to cry. I shed a few tears, spoke to my mom, and told her what happened and hung up the phone. As I drove home, I felt like a failure, and I felt like I failed my son, family, friends, and Commander.

All of that commuting felt like it was for nothing. Here I was trying to build a secure future for my son but felt like it was denied. I said to myself when plan A doesn't work kick in plan B. I continued to move forward with my military career. It brought stability and excitement, but I continued to move forward. Two years before retirement, I received a phone call with an opportunity for a position I was not looking for. I considered this my dream assignment I can work independently, and work two days from home. I knew right then, and there this was the opportunity where I could pursue my degree again.

I remember someone telling me that I could not do both, but I had to decide which one I wanted. Reflecting now on what happened back then, I realized that God could see down through the eons of time, let him direct your path, and you can never go wrong. I am now at a place where I am ready to submit my application for the nursing program. God's timing is not our timing; trust the process. Delay is not denial. Walk-in due season, and you will see all of your dreams come to come to manifestation.

Cashina Smith

FEBRUARY 10

Prayer List

Take the time to pray for others today and put their names below

_____

_____

_____

_____

_____

_____

_____

_____

_____

_____

_____

_____

_____

_____

_____

_____

_____

FEBRUARY 11

Rejoice always, pray continually, give thanks in all circumstances; for this is God's will for you in Christ Jesus.

1 Thessalonians 5:16-18

FEBRUARY 12

I am led by
my faith in
the Lord

FEBRUARY 13

I am filled
with God's
love

FEBRUARY 14

DECLARATION: I decree and declare that I have overcome a life of low self-esteem.

AFFIRMATION: I am free and alright with myself!

God fearfully and wonderfully makes us, yet we are often tainted by our experiences in life to the point they slowly condition us to become who we are not meant to be. Growing up in the fast lane as some say, I found myself on a road of destruction: teen runaway (+self-inflicted homelessness), alcohol abuse, school suspension and physical abuse to name a few. What hurt most were the words I overheard people said about me, statements like "she'll never amount to anything, she's a prostitute, and she had an abortion." I already thought little of myself, and then to overhear the negative comments just butchered my already diminished self-esteem. No, I was never a prostitute nor had an abortion, but the picture I had painted by my wild behavior overshadowed any truths. I offered no self-defense about the incorrect assumptions; instead, I coped in silence and continued living rebelliously. My hard exterior hid a young girl who just wanted to know she was beautiful and had worth.

I managed to graduate high school, join the military, and fortunately marry a wonderful man. Within three years, I then had a near fatal horseback riding accident that left me with multiple injuries and a derailed bodybuilding career. I was emotionally devastated. Low self-esteem, ugly scars, and new marriage...do I cope by silence again? No, not this time for I had the Lord on my side! This new way of thinking wasn't immediate, as I had to learn to walk again and accept my condition, include the scars and the hard fact that I would never compete as a professional bodybuilder. I wasn't happy, but angry with God that my scared leg held me back from competition. I eventually realized that bodybuilding had given me a false allusion of well-being and true gratefulness for God's creation—ME! It was in preparation of this writing that I realized I hadn't used any Declarations and Affirmations to overcome low self-esteem. I am amazed of this discovery and confirmation, as the foundational scripture for the ministry I founded in 2010 is Psalm 139:14, Fearfully & Wonderfully Made by God!

If I could go back and say anything to that young girl inside me, it would be "you are beautiful, and you have worth". I would encourage her not to let her condition and the harsh words people spoke about her define who she is in life. With all wisdom I would inspire her not to be silent, but to speak up and proclaim her worth. In great humility I would only look down on her to offer my hand to lift her, develop strategy to overcome, and walk it out with her. I would reassure her that even in her struggle to live right, that the Lord is still calling her name! Finally, I want to encourage you to affirm yourself with your voice, "I AM FREE AND ALRIGHT WITH MYSELF, BECAUSE GOD FEARFULLY AND WONDERFULLY MADE ME!

Janie Church

FEBRUARY 15

So then, just as you received Christ Jesus as Lord, continue to live your lives in him, rooted and built up in him, strengthened in the faith as you were taught, and overflowing with thankfulness.

Colossians 2:6-7

FEBRUARY 16

I am humble in whom God has made me

I am a leaving my comfort zone behind me!

FEBRUARY 18

DECLARATION: I decree and declare that I will not be bitter, I will be better, and I will turn from being fearful into being fearless.

AFFIRMATION: I am an extraordinary woman who turns the ordinary into extraordinary by taking extra measures to apply strength, compassion, patience, and love in all that I do.

What makes a woman extraordinary? She is unique in many ways, her strength, compassion, patience, perseverance, resilience, and love. In the early 2000s, I was in a toxic relationship, which included infidelity and domestic violence. My ex was arrested for domestic violence against myself and my children, and while in jail, he attended prison ministry and gave his life to Christ. When he was released, he began to fellowship at the ministry and started to pursue me again. I also began to attend the ministry and then gave my life to Christ. Within that time, my ex and I got married, and then the drama started all over again. My ex backslid into his old ways and left me for another woman who was very close to my family and me. I was so lost and confused. I couldn't understand why this was happening to me, and I couldn't understand how the people I loved could hurt and betray me. I left the world; the drinking, fornicating, and getting high, and now I am serving and worshiping God. How does this happen? I kept asking God why, and I heard the voice of God say, "Why not? Why not you, Leslie"? Have you ever gotten to the point where you had to ask God why this was happening?

I thought about it and realized while I was praying for the Lord to change my ex, I realized God wanted to change me, that there was a purpose, a plan, and a path he has for me. So, my prayer changed Lord make me better, a better woman, better wife, better mother, better daughter, and a better friend. I let go of what was in the past. I began to look forward to what God had designed and purposed for me in my future. After being abused and put down for so long, realizing that I am an extraordinary woman took declaration, prayer, and pulling on the Holy Spirit to guide and protect me in all that I say and do. Every day I intentionally make up in my mind and in my Spirit to give extra in everything. I am intentional when communicating to be a positive reinforcement in someone's life. You don't know what someone else is going through. I walk in love and compassion, always giving and caring for those in need and being the light in someone's dark. Having patience and strength go hand and hand, just knowing that we are a long way from being perfect, and we all have our flaws to being mindful of extending grace to others just like grace was extended to me.

Dear extraordinary woman, we create the atmosphere that we live in, and you, too, can be a remarkable woman. Intentional woman today makes the ordinary extraordinary. Be Extra! Extra Strength! Extra Compassion! Extra Patience! Extra Perseverance! Extra Resilience! Extra Love!

Leslie Foster

FEBRUARY 19

Encouragement

Take the time to encourage yourself today. Write down your wins for the month!

_____
_____
_____
_____
_____
_____
_____
_____
_____
_____
_____
_____
_____
_____
_____

FEBRUARY 20

Let the peace of Christ rule in your hearts, since as members of one body you were called to peace. And be thankful. Let the message of Christ dwell among you richly as you teach and admonish one another with all wisdom through psalms, hymns, and songs from the Spirit, singing to God with gratitude in your hearts. And whatever you do, whether in word or deed, do it all in the name of the Lord Jesus, giving thanks to God the Father through him.

Colossians 3:15-17

FEBRUARY 21

DECLARATION: I decree and declare that that I will no longer carry the weight of rejection because my portion is the complete, undeniable love and acceptance of God.

AFFIRMATION: I am loved and accepted.

No one likes rejection. Belonging is an innate and inherent human need. If we're honest, we can all remember at least one time when we experienced rejection and how it made us feel. My crush on "Victor" was undeniable. I was a 12-year-old, 7th grader; "Victor" and I had been friends throughout elementary school and loved talking on the phone. The day I summoned up the courage to write a note declaring my feelings was the same day that he called, saying he only liked me as a friend. When I asked him "why," he said I wasn't his type. He answered my skin was too dark; he liked girls with lighter skin. He confessed his "love" for a mutual friend and asked if I could hook him up. I felt devastated. His comments reopened a wound inflicted by other children calling me names like "tar baby;" it reminded me that having dark skin wasn't in!

Rejection is a nasty weapon used by the enemy to strip us of our identity, teach us self-hatred, steal our self-esteem, and instill the lie that we are not good enough. If you've been told you were an unwanted pregnancy, you were not planned, or there was a hope that you were another gender, the enemy has used those words to create a narrative of rejection while you were still in your mother's womb. Subsequently, it shows up in our personal and professional lives. My struggle with rejection peaked in my late 20's after becoming a Minister. My interactions with others revealed I was suffering from the residual effects of rejection: mistrust, inability to receive love, fear of giving love, guarded, and an entrenched doubt about God's love for me. Four strategies played a role in my liberation: (1) intercession, (2) ministry of deliverance, (3) counseling, and (4) intimacy with God. My spiritual mother interceded for me, provided spiritual counseling, and led me in one-on-one deliverance sessions.

She counseled me using God's word and taught me the truth: I am loved and accepted. I did intentional and ongoing work to remove emotional clutter, thereby making room for deeper intimacy with God. I secured a therapist, prayed, and studied God's word, specifically scriptures that told me who I am in Christ. Each day, I put on the spiritual armor referenced in Ephesians 6:11-18 to combat the enemy's attacks on my heart and mind. Rejection is a natural part of the human experience. Everyone will not like or accept us. Yet, God wants us to experience his wraparound love and unconditional acceptance. Continually, He will send people to our lives who love and accept us. For every rejection, there is always acceptance. Therefore, when we experience rejection, we have confidence that it does not have the power to defeat us, silence us, or make us feel small. Through Christ, we have victory over rejection, and we bask, abide, and thrive in the love of God, which flows to us through those divinely sent into our lives.

Dr. Synetheia Newby

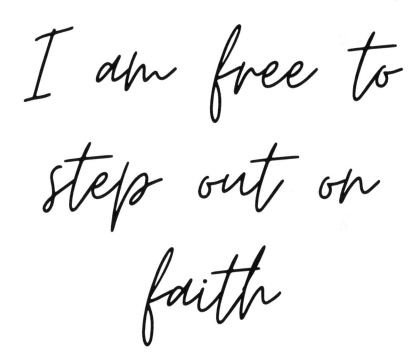

I am free to step out on faith

I am

supportive of

others

FEBRUARY 24

DECLARATION: I decree and declare that I can and will use the voice, skills, and talents that God has given me.

AFFIRMATION: I am here to seek and create crowning moments through the Glory of God!

Crowning moments are defined as taking intentional and actionable steps to reach a desirable goal or outcome. For such a long time, I had been seeking: new opportunities a unique role in other companies to align myself with organizations that valued diversity, inclusion a belonging attempting to be adequately compensated trying to share how I was qualified seeking to find someone that will consider my transferrable skills, seeking a new place to learn, grow and develop only to realize that I had the power to create the life I desired I got caught up in finding and trying to force my way into spaces and places that I did not realize that God wanted me to count and cultivate the things that He made in me and not let the world define me.

I was told that I was unqualified, did not know what I was doing, I did not have the skills and knowledge, and to rethink what I wanted to do. God said I already told you, stay the course. After being told these things consistently, I decided to imagine what would create the crowning moment for me. I started to connect with individuals who were doing the things that I desired to do, follow them, have coffee with them, study the industry, and learn all that I could learn. Then one day, it happened. The shift came, the release came, I was laid off. The layoff was leveling me up. God leveled up my creativity, my home, and my friendships. People will tell you what is best for you based on their limited experiences. God will tell you what is best for you based on his limitless power and plan for your life! It's not about us but what God wants to do through us.

The world may count you out, but God is always counting you in. He had calculated all the gifts, skills, and experiences before you were born. Will you take the time to tune out the world and tune in to the word of God? I decided to tune into the word of God. The world may change; people may change, but God is the same yesterday, today, and forever. God wants to crown us with His steadfast love and mercy, and because of that, I not only seek crowning moments, I look for opportunities to create them.

TEdra Jackson

FEBRUARY 25

DECLARATION: I decree and declare that my prayers echo from the Earth to the heavens.

AFFIRMATION: I am a supernatural sound machine.

The loudest sound in history came from a volcanic eruption on an island in Indonesia called Krakatoa in 1883. The eruption was so loud that it could be heard thousands of miles away. Sound travels in waves through the air. As we speak, the words we say travel to far off places that we cannot see. After we have spoken our words, and sometimes even forgotten what we have said, our words are released into the atmosphere to accomplish the specific thing that we have sent them to do. The Bible says to be anxious for nothing but to pray about everything. When we speak our prayers to our Father, He hears us, no matter how faint the cry or enormous the roar. The call of your prayers can penetrate even the hardest places in your life and create an echo into the heavenly realm. When we speak the Word of God to our circumstances, our words refract, moving from the natural world, and transforming into a spiritual weapon.

 A few years back, I faced some relationship challenges. I knew that God was using my pain to push me into a deeper prayer life. However, I was worried about what God would think about my selfish motives. I wanted what I wanted! I had always had a hard time seeing God as loving and gentle. I saw Him as a Judge who was going to get me for disobedience and living the way I wanted to live. However, as I began to fast and pray over my situation, my view slowly changed. I began to understand the power that my prayers held, not only to change my situation but to transform my relationship and view of God. As the Holy Spirit taught me to pray the Word of God and use the scriptures that He specifically led me to, my trust in Him grew like never before.

I learned to pray powerfully for change. My prayer life erupted and even spilled over onto my job. I began openly interceding for others, which is something I was always afraid to do. There I was, standing in a circle, praying for a group of my co-workers, praying for their marriages, praying for their children, praying for their finances, praying for their peace, out loud and unashamed. I was using my voice as a weapon, a powerful sound, for God's kingdom. It was not for me, but His people. Not only did my situation change, so did those of my co-workers. Prayer can go places that we can never go ourselves.

Not by might, nor by power, but by His Spirit (Zachariah 4:6). Today, I challenge you to believe that you can pray prayers that will be heard worldwide, echoing from Earth to heaven. Use the roar that God has given you.

Dr. Xaviera Robinson

FEBRUARY 26

Devote yourselves to prayer, being watchful and thankful.

Colossians 4:2

I trust the
Lord's plans
that He has
for my life

FEBRUARY 28

Prayer List

Take the time to pray for others today and put their
names below

_____

_____

_____

_____

_____

_____

_____

_____

_____

_____

_____

_____

_____

Delight yourself in the Lord, and he will give you the desires of your heart. Commit your way to the Lord; trust in him, and he will act.

Psalm 37:4-5

March

MARCH 1

Goal Setting

Use today to set your goals for the year.
Be clear and specific with what you want to achieve.
Break the goal down into steps.
All the best in achieving your goals this year!

I am grateful
and blessed to
be in my
current position

We will celebrate each other more than we criticize!

MARCH 4

When I walked down the aisle on my wedding day, thoughts of getting a divorce were not on my mind. Actually, on the contrary, we planned to spend the rest of our lives together and grow old together. Due to circumstances beyond my control and some within my control, the painful experience of divorcing the person I loved, began. It seemed like one day I was walking down the aisle, and then another day, I was walking to the post office to retrieve the divorce documents sent to me. As I signed my name on the divorce documents, the pain of shame overshadowed me. Shame causes us to ask questions; "How could I face my friends and family with this failed marriage? What do I say to my young children, who will grow up without their father around the house? How will I explain why I am now a single mom? Could I have done something different to save my marriage? How do I face my accusers, those who will charge me with the guilt of not staying in a mentally and emotionally abusive marriage? How will I face the people who will see me as a failure?" Shame will also cause us to believe we are the worst of all, sinners.

When we ask a question, most of the time, it is to gain information. But when Jesus, our all-knowing Savior, asks a question, it is to bring revelation and insight. In John 8, Jesus asked a woman, who was caught in adultery, a question in order to bring revelation to her life. He asked her, "Where are your accusers?" If she hadn't done anything wrong, then this question would be meaningless. But this young lady was dragged into the presence of Jesus by the religious leaders who caught her in the act of adultery. She could not hide from what she did or deny what had happened because she was caught in the middle of her sin. The religious leaders didn't realize they brought her to the right place, at the right time to encounter the right person. So how do we handle the pain of shame and move on with our lives? How do we face people who may choose to condemn us, instead of comforting us?

Jesus' encounter with the woman caught in adultery gives us insight about how to handle the pain of shame and to silence the accusers. Jesus told the woman she has no accusers because everyone has sinned; we all fall short of God's glorious standard. Freedom from shame comes when you know you have no accusers. You have no one qualified to charge you with shortcomings because no one is free of their failures and sins. God has a rescue plan for your life, and His name is Jesus.

So the next time shame grips your heart and causes you to hide, ponder on the words of Jesus, "Where are your accusers?" Then gently reply, "I have none!"

Shawn Young-Smith

I declare that today will be a good day!

Therefore, since we are receiving a kingdom that cannot be shaken, let us be thankful, and so worship God acceptably with reverence and awe, for our "God is a consuming fire."

Hebrews 12:28-29

MARCH 7

DECLARATION: I decree and declare that I am strong enough to face any situation that comes my way.

AFFIRMATION: I am someone that God can trust with trouble.

I remember when I was lying in a hospital bed and felt as though I was slipping away, and all I could do was mutter under my breath: "Thank you for trusting me with trouble." It helped me stay calm and remember that I could go through it because the God of Heaven trusted me to handle it well. I had become someone that God could trust with trouble, and it gave me comfort and strength.

Often, we go through things in life, and we often don't understand why. Sometimes we might feel as though God is picking on us. We may ask ourselves, "Why am I the one going through this trouble." What makes the difference is how we look at it. God does not pick on any of His children; He loves us. What He does do is select us to walk the path of situations. It's in those situations that He demonstrates His trust in us. In other words, God trusts us with trouble! The Bible tells us in 1 Corinthians 10:13 that God will not put more on us than we can bear. So, when we find ourselves in challenging positions. He trusted that we could take it. That with His help, we could not only get through it but bring glory to His name at the end of it. Knowing this helps us to maintain the right attitude while in the process.

Becoming someone that God can trust with trouble happens when we realize that our problems aren't about us. It's an opportunity for us to recognize that it's really about someone else. That sister that will cross our path later in life that needs to see what victory looks like to have hope that God can be glorified in her situation at the end like He was in ours. God has a plan for each of us that includes breaking some things off and imparting others, but they don't happen through osmosis. Often there will be a source of discomfort that we must walk out with God for His result to manifest in our lives. It requires a life event or "trouble" to get us there. When we are faced with these challenges, we can change our perspective from "why me" into "Wow, God, you trust me with this." It becomes such an honor and humbling experience when we realize that God thought enough of us to go through that test. We must remember that God made us and knows the investment that He has on the inside of us, even when we don't.

Whatever we've gone through, God trusted us with it. Whatever we will go through in the future, it will be that God entrusted us with it. Let's be the type of woman that God can trust to go through and come out better rather than bitter.

Cureene Benefield

<u>MARCH 8</u>

I am more
than
enough

I am set free from all things that hold me back

Through Jesus, therefore, let us continually offer to God a sacrifice of praise — the fruit of lips that openly profess his name. And do not forget to do good and to share with others, for with such sacrifices God is pleased.

Hebrews 15:13-16

MARCH 11

DECLARATION: I decree and declare that I will stand with my head held high with correct thoughts about who I am, and I choose to ignore every other voice in disagreement with His voice.

AFFIRMATION: I am listening to God's voice, and I agree with what God says.

When thinking about what my heart would like to share with you immediately, two subjects came to mind, First the importance of balance. I am so addicted to being on this constant quest for obtaining that steady feeling in the ups and downs of life. Knowing that He can give us a peace which passes all understanding, there are still times I feel like I am on a hamster wheel, running with all I got in the same spot while time is just doing what it does. It became a tug of war between the balance conversation, and then the journey of motherhood resonated loudly also. I had hoped to have that picture of love, marriage, and
then the baby in the baby carriage. My first love turned into first loves, and then I realized maybe they never really loved me at all. My happier story came out of order and becoming a young single mother of two children from two different men.

No one expected I would be a single mother in a million years from my image throughout my childhood. I carried myself in a humble, respectful, polite manner; however, I had my curiosities and brokenness. I tried to fill with relationships that were self-invoked, and the enemy would use me against me with cycles meant for my demise. I dealt with disappointment in myself, simultaneously surviving an ultra-abusive relationship, eventually being left to raise them while having one old enough to witness terrible things. I planned my strategic exit and chose to let God be my Father, Leader, and Restorer. He healed me 100,000 percent, and I recovered from the heartbreak. God aided in breaking chains of nursing a victim mentality. While leaving NO residue of unforgiveness and bitterness, I finally have peace, and I'm obsessed with God's loyalty. I was not prepared for my past decisions to haunt me through my seed. The oldest, which saw too much and bore the weight of an oppressive invisible atmosphere, ate the fruit of my uncertainties. I realized as she began to grow, familiar thought patterns I had survived now taunted her. I started watching the enemy attempt what he could not accomplish with my life through hers. The pain is indescribable, but there's a reality that my survival taught me, which I want to encourage you today.

No matter what life looks like, how people may judge, you may have forgotten your value and dignity. God didn't. He already provided your exit from brokenness and lies. Nor does your worth diminish. You have a choice to change your mind and stand in Him again and again. I wanted to encourage someone in a dark place when feeling humiliated, rejected, and when you forget you matter that you are priceless. There is a fight for your peace and sanity, which has already been won. Your life is meaningful and matters to God.

Angel Jarrell

I declare that
I will always
stay true to
myself

MARCH 13

DECLARATION: I decree and declare that my voice will be used for the purpose that it was intended for.

AFFIRMATION: My voice is powerful; my words have meaning. I am a voice of influential change.

We will not use our voices to waste words, speak words of negativity, speak words that degrade, or spread hate. We will instead be voices of life, love, healing, encouragement, acknowledging that what and how speak has a universal power to change the course of life. I first realized how powerful words were in 2011. I had an accident in my then 1996 Honda Accord. The insurance money received as a result of the accident was enough to pay off this bill that I had been declaring I was going to pay off. The next time I realized how powerful words could be, was with the birth of my son in 2017.

After a difficult labor and delivery with my daughter, I began declaring that if I ever had another child, the labor would be quick, I wouldn't need a c-section and there would be no hospital bills. He came a whole month early, too tiny to even think about a c-section, took me five minutes to push him out, and there were no medical bills because I had Medicaid due to having no income. It hit me some months after each of these events, how much power our words and thoughts can possess. I was amazed because I didn't think about this power even after reading in the bible how much power the tongue has. I was also able to examine how much negativity I had spoken over my life over the years. You know those moments when we say what won't happen, practicing self-doubt, rehearsing words that others have spoken over us, or declaring that we can't make it. I had a lot of those moments and still do when I get overwhelmed.

Nevertheless, we must dig deep. I do my best to speak what I want to see in my life but also to consider what I'm asking or praying for because Lord knows I didn't want to have to go through that accident to pay off a bill or to have to lose a job to have no medical bills. Our words and our voices are so important and influential. We must make sure we are doing our part to speak light into a world filled with so much darkness. Weigh your words, prayers, declarations, because once they let loose from your lips, there is no taking them back. Steer clear from speaking anything that degrades or is just plain negative.

It will not be easy because we are faced with situations daily where the things, we want to say are not influential, encouraging, or positive. I encourage you to strive to be a voice of light and speak words of light. Be intentional about it and practice one day at a time. You will not only feel better but also see the rewards of your intent when you least expect it.

Stephanie Banks

MARCH 14

When the peace of Christ rules in our hearts, thankfulness overflows. Even in the darkest of times, we can praise God for his love, his sovereignty, and his promise to be near us when we call

Psalms 145:18

MARCH 15

Encouragement

Take the time to encourage yourself today. Write down your
wins for the month!

_____

_____

_____

_____

_____

_____

_____

_____

_____

_____

_____

_____

_____

_____

_____

_____

I declare that God aligns my heart, actions and desires

MARCH 17

DECLARATION: I declare that I have the power to encourage others with the words I speak.

AFFIRMATION: I am planting seeds of encouragement in the words I speak!

When I lived with my abusive husband, I became very bitter with the world. All I ever heard was negativity and hate. I got so conditioned to that environment that I carried it with me everywhere I went. It was very depressing and exhausting! After 14 years of marriage, I left. It was the best thing I could have done for myself and my children. I needed counseling for what I had experienced, and for the unforgiveness, I was feeling for myself and my husband. It took a long time to heal, forgive, and, most importantly, love myself again. During the whole process, I learned a precious lesson: Words are like seeds.

When you speak something out, you are giving life to what you are saying. The seeds you plant cultivate within each person. Your words bring life to those seeds. Speaking kindness and grace to others have a positive impact on your own life. God encourages us to plant seeds of encouragement whenever we speak.

Think of it this way; we are each farmers for God. As we plant those seeds of encouragement, our words and our actions sow the seeds. Our actions are the soil that covers the words we use. Our words of encouragement, love, and grace are the fertilizer that grows the seeds and blossoms. Before you know it, your one little seed of encouragement cultivated into a beautiful garden filled with God's beauty.

If we want grace, we must extend grace and mercy in our words. If we want wisdom, share words of wisdom with others. We have to choose to use words that will empower others, not hinder them. God lives within us, and He uses us as instruments to plant and harvest seeds in other people. Our words can be the glue that holds a relationship together. When we speak the word of God and use words that encourage others, we please Him. He continues to give us the tools we need to harvest the garden.

Remember this; when we build up each other with our words of encouragement, we build ourselves up too. Through my journey, I have learned the weight that my words have. I love speaking words of encouragement as much as I can. It helps the person I am speaking to, but it makes me feel so good inside. I am happier and less stressed because I know that my seeds of encouragement bring happiness to others.

What seeds of encouragement are you going to plant today?

Nancy Gonzalez

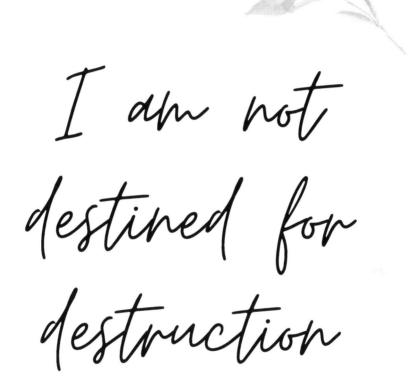

I am not destined for destruction

MARCH 19

I declare
that no
weapon formed
against me
shall prosper

For the Lord gives wisdom; from his mouth come knowledge and understanding.

Proverbs 2:6

MARCH 21

DECLARATION: I decree and declare that through the will of the LORD that I will remain accountable for standing steadfast in my purpose.

AFFIRMATION: I am the mission.

Remaining fulfilled in your purpose is essential to your core foundation. Knowing who you are and being confident about taking the steps needed to change your life trajectory is critical, especially if you are not quite where you want to be in life. In the past, I have accepted positions in life that I knew ultimately were not my right assignment, but I took on specific roles because it appeared to be the right choice at the time. There came the point in my life where I had grown tired of the career path I had taken. From the outside looking in, I was excelling, but I was empty. I was growing as a leader, and I managed a team over multiple facilities. However, I was emotionally and mentally stagnant. Honestly, I was going through the motions, all while losing me in the process. I was losing a grip on whom I wanted to be as a woman. It was during this time in my life that I had to refocus and redirect the mission.

In the summer of 2019, I decided I had to take control of my path and where I wanted to be in life. Consequently, I decided to leap, and I chose to live in my truth. My truth entailed me trying something new. I allowed myself to be open to the possibilities beyond what was
right in front of me. Trust me, leaving behind almost 14 years of familiarity for something new was extremely difficult. The hardest part of it all was that this new job required me to leave my son and husband behind while I transitioned to a different state.

I had never left my family for more than a few days at a time. This new position would require me to be gone even longer, and although the move was not too far from home, being without them each night was heartbreaking and lonely at times.

Nevertheless, during this time of solitude and reflection, I rediscovered me. I revealed to myself just how strong I was. Redirecting the mission proved to be burdensome at first glance, but despite the challenges I faced, the opportunity led to a better me. When you find yourself in a situation that no longer rightfully serves you, when you seem to have lost yourself or do not feel satisfied with whom you have become, it is time to refocus and redirect the mission.

Purpose is defined as the reason something is created or for which something exists. Waking up each day and doing what you love is a fantastic thing. So, ask yourself what makes you most happy? Walkthrough this day knowing you are the mission. Let it be a goal each day that you are the mission and that you will remain accomplished and complete.

Windi Floyd-Reynolds

MARCH 22

Prayer List

Take the time to pray for others today and put their names below

_____

_____

_____

_____

_____

_____

_____

_____

_____

_____

_____

_____

_____

_____

MARCH 23

DECLARATION: I decree and declare that God is doing a new thing in me. He is the light for my path and has made all my crooked paths straight.

AFFIRMATION: I am powerful, resilient, and predestined to succeed in every endeavor within God's will for my life.

I have always been a dreamer. I did not always know how I was going to accomplish my goals and dreams, but I trusted that I would. My testimony of faith began over 25 years ago. I wanted to attend the University of South Florida as a high school senior (the only school I applied to). Might I add, I didn't receive an acceptance letter to attend until two weeks before the start of the Fall semester.

Have you have ever felt so confident and at peace with a situation, and you did not understand why? My dear friend, you were/are under the covering of God; it is the Holy Spirit interceding for you. So, here is a fact, faith is necessary even when you have no idea of how that feeling deep within your gut will come to fruition. Before I was accepted to USF, I spoke and affirmed that I was going and that I would be in attendance in the Fall. I told everyone. It was a defining moment that was dependent on a God that I could not see (faith). I had no idea what God was about to do, but there was a constant movement in my spirit, a nudge that I could not explain that gave me peace.

Have you had a nudge in your spirit that promotes you to keep believing despite your current circumstances? Are you listening? The dream of attending college, moving away from home for the first time, was God's way of creating a real need for Him and Him alone. During my freshman year at USF, I began to experience a deep yearning for God. I was raised in a Christian household, baptized at the age of seven, but I had never had a personal relationship with God. I would find myself lying in my dorm room many nights, imploring God for more.

God doesn't delay; campus disciples quickly approached me for one full year before I accepted an invitation to have a personal bible study. That lead to me learning what God expected from my life and how to live for Him. I decided to receive a second baptism, and that started my renewed relationship with Jesus Christ. I challenge you to remember God and His promises and remember all the answered prayers that you have already received. My acceptance letter into college was the first step toward a life full of hope and complete reliance on God. Had I given up hope and stopped believing and pursuing my dream of college, who knows where I might be. It had to happen that way; it was not a careless mistake (applying to one university), but rather a step directed by God all along.

Listen to God's whisper, the nudge in your spirit that wants to direct your path. You have greatness within you; let God show you more than you could ever think or imagine possible. I believe in you, and I am praying for you.

Catrena Giles

MARCH 24

DECLARATION: I decree and declare that God's character is a blessing in my life exceedingly abundantly above anything I can ask or think.

AFFIRMATION: I am in great expectation of God's best to manifest in every area of my life.

Several years ago, I used my authority and stretched my FAITH, seeking what then seemed like the impossible. I was in graduate school and renting a room. I was grateful for a space to lay my head, pray, and maintain peace. My prayer was that I would have my apartment. At the time, I was not working at all, and I was a full-time student. In the natural, one would say, I had a limited source of income. It looked impossible for me to move on my own. I wanted to live my life from God's plan and see things from His perspective and promises. I stood on the promises, and I believed that I would see God's best for me, manifested in my life. After two years of moving around and sharing living spaces with others. I stepped out on my faith and began my search for an apartment. I started my apartment search based on the rental cost, which was not in my desired location to live.

After visiting a duplex apartment, I decided to submit an application and fees. On the day I was prepared to submit my application, I was reminded of my prayer, I was expecting God's best in every area of my life. I was prompted to reflect on my prayer and to give thought to God's promises. I heard a small voice ask me, "I thought you wanted my best in every area of your life?" I was limiting God; I was making decisions based on my ability. I was putting limitations on what I thought I could receive based on me, and not what God could do on my behalf. Recognizing I was operating from a place of lack, I quickly made an adjustment in my plans, called and canceled my interest in renting the duplex.

Shortly after that, I was in the area that I desired to live. I walked into the leasing office and inquired about the availability to rent a two-bedroom apartment. The leasing agent replied if I qualified, I could move in within the next two weeks. I submitted an application and the fees. I was approved for the apartment. Our Father kept His promise to me. He not only opened the door for me but secured the apartment and made a way for me to pay the rent for several months in advance. I renewed my lease three times and completed my graduate degree studies while living in the apartment.

Father, we thank you for everything that we need you have already provided for us through the gift of the "the blood" of the finished works of Jesus Christ. We are reminded when we pray, we must believe, and receive, and we shall have what we prayed for. We praise your name, Father. We will see the manifestation of God's blessings and favor in our lives because the word of God will not be returned to Him void. God is a keeper of His promises to His children.

Angelette Verdena-King

I am not destined for destruction

If any of you lacks wisdom, you should ask God, who gives generously to all without finding fault, and it will be given to you.

James 1:5

MARCH 27

DECLARATION: I decree and declare that it's not over until God says it's over. Man has a report and God has a report, and God's report supersedes man's report.

AFFIRMATION: I am child of God, set apart to do his will. Nothing and no one can take us out of God's hand, not even death. I will trust him at all cost regardless of what I face.

On September 25, 2018 my husband got up experiencing very strong indigestion. He initially asked me to go get him some antacid medicine, so I went and brought them back to him. Once I reached him, he then asked me to take him to the hospital instead. An EKG was done on him and he was hooked up to an IV. Once the IV was emptied, he felt much better and wanted to go home. The doctor came in and told us that his results detected that he had three blockages in his arteries. The doctor recommended a triple bypass or three stents to be implanted. He said the stent procedure would be less invasive than the triple bypass and it should only take about 1 ½ hours to perform. The operation started at 3:30 PM. Around 6:00 PM I heard over the intercom, code blue to room 228 three times. The third call alarmed me, since that was the room he had been in prior to the surgery.

My sweet husband was rushed to the operating room. The doctors put him in a medically induced coma to save his life. He was returned to the ICU and not given much of a chance to survive. We were told that he would likely not make it through the night. My mind did not know how to register this news, and wanted to go into panic mode. All of a sudden my spirit cried, "wake-up and fight!" I heard God say, do you trust me? So, I arose from my stupor and started declaring the Word of God over his life. I declared that he would live and not die! I began to plead the blood of Jesus over his life. I prayed like I had never prayed before. Our church family and my family prayed through the night. The doctors told us that it would take about 54 days for the paralyzing drugs to wear off. Then they said that he would need a trek inserted to allow him to breathe. They kept him for two weeks, reporting a grim outcome to which we refused to receive.

On October 18, 2018, his coma induced body was transported to another hospital. My daughter and I stayed with him day in and day out, speaking life over his seemingly lifeless body. We fought and were determined to see God's healing manifest in his body. On December 5, 2018 my husband moved his index finger. It was the sign we had been waiting to see, though we still had to fight the negative reports with the word of God daily. On January 18, 2019 to the doctor's surprise, my love was transferred to Tampa General's Rehab facility, where he stayed and worked his way back to walking and functioning on his own. He left that facility on April 3, 2019 and on the road to a full recovery. We couldn't have done it without daily prayer and the hand of God having mercy on us and favoring us.

Psalms 91 has been my go to scripture since then and I want to encourage you to read it when you are dealing with tough times in your life.

Mary Banks

My life is abundant and it continues to grow

How much better to get wisdom than gold, to get insight rather than silver!

Proverbs 16:16

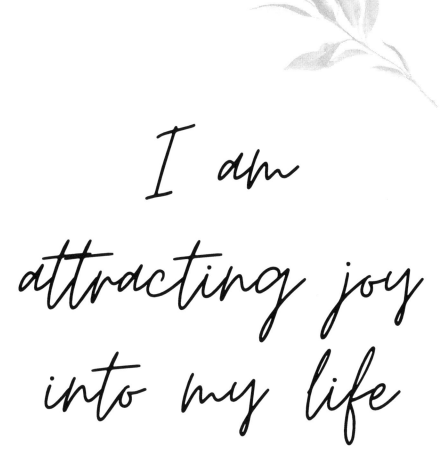

I am
attracting joy
into my life

I am calm
and content
with my life

April

APRIL 1

Goal Setting

Use today to set your goals for the year.
Be clear and specific with what you want to achieve.
Break the goal down into steps.
All the best in achieving your goals this year!

APRIL 2

DECLARATION: I decree and declare that peace and comfort are upon me.

AFFIRMATION: I am created with the purpose of God's peace and favor abound me.

From January to March 2014, I went through what I thought was the worst few weeks of my life. I found myself asking, why? How could God let these things happen to me? Is God listening to my prayers? Why am I here? No one will miss me. In a few week's spans of time, I lost my uncle to a sudden heart attack and my father to cancer. I was in a toxic marriage and a custody and child support battle with my children's father. I worked full time and was enrolled in a leadership development course for promotion. At the same time, I was struggling to complete the last semester of my bachelor's degree. I was stressed to the max and felt like I couldn't take anymore. I felt so empty.

Despite having grown up in church and understanding how God was supposed to work, I didn't have a genuine relationship with my heavenly father. After a few weeks, everything started to spiral out of control. I started having horrible thoughts. I felt like I was drowning in a crowded pool, and no one stopped or tried to save me. All I could think of was wanting to see my father and hear his voice. One morning at the end of March 2014, I woke up in a fog and thought the pain would stop today. I swallowed a handful of every pill in my medicine cabinet, saw my children off to school, and my then, husband off to work. I laid back down in my bed and cried myself to sleep while praying never to wake up.

My family found me and rushed me to the emergency room. While I was asleep, I had a warm feeling come over me, and I hear a whisper in my ear say, "your steps are ordered, and I am not done with you." I started waking up and could hear my previous pastor praying over me. God was speaking to me through him, and all I could do was cry. He continued to pray with me for my strength, and most importantly, for me to be able to forgive myself for making such a horrible choice. He left me with some words of encouragement, and I knew I wasn't alone. I felt like a new person. My relationship with my family grew stronger. I began tithing, serving, and praying regularly. I found beautiful new friendships. My relationship with God was changing before my eyes.

God blessed me to finish my bachelor's degree and my leadership program. Within a couple of months at work, I received the first of four promotions. He delivered me from that toxic, unhealthy marriage. I was favored with a new marriage and another child. All of my children are blessed and flourishing. Thanks be to God. We know firsthand that God is a miracle worker; He uses our lives to be a light for others. We are walking testimonies. My sister God can do all things. Just trust him. He's got you!

Jovoni Williams

I give myself
space to learn

APRIL 4

DECLARATION: I decree and declare that I was designed with a purpose, and I will operate in the truth of who I am.

AFFIRMATION: I am a powerful woman of God who has embraced all God has uniquely created me to be.

Control is determining what someone else does, whether they choose to or not disregarding others' feelings to accomplish one's agenda. Control is so real. I've never been controlled by a man before; only my mother. It makes me feel so helpless. I wouldn't say I like that feeling. I despise and detest it. My mother had such a hold on my spirit; it drove me to the point of hate. Here I am finally free from one dictator, and I've allowed another to come in and imprison me in a worse way. It took me years to heal from her torment. I want to recover from this. As a child, I'd pretend I had a warm, loving mother who cared about my feelings. Now with him, I imagine that he loves me. I play meaningless words through my mind to give me some sense of peace. It often doesn't work, but I keep trying. I've allowed Satan to enter my mind and take advantage of my insecurities. He knows exactly what to do, and I often forget how to defeat him. My prayer is, "God, I need your help. Better yet, please do this completely. I ask for wisdom but rarely know when you're speaking.

Please help me to know your voice so I may allow your will. Please heal my heart. It's so broken, and it's been for a while now. That's such a wretched feeling. I don't think I acknowledge it as such. But it's so real. I need your jumbo band-aid. Please fill the spaces and recreate me. Amen". I wish I could say that I found my voice that day in June of 2008 but it took another five years before my true boldness would emerge. My therapist challenged me to spend some real-time with God. Things had gotten so bad I couldn't hear Him anymore. When I finally stilled myself, I heard him say, "Trust me." That was so much easier said than done. I had been filled with shame and hopelessness for so long; I didn't even recognize myself in the mirror. Control and narcissism had once again found their way into the inner depths of my heart disguised as someone I loved. I had lost myself. I asked God for a band-aid. But what I needed was reconstructive open-heart surgery. God wanted to cut me open and restore all the places that had been destroyed. I pleaded with God to introduce me to me, the person He had created me to be. God showed me that I am a prophet. I have a voice that is meant to deliver His words to the people.

I am a prophet of God. Prophets are courageous and confident, comfortable standing alone, and they stand out in crowds. When they speak, people listen. He intentionally designed me this way on purpose with purpose. He's intentionally designed you too. Together, we will find our voices and boldly speak the words that He places inside our hearts. It's time to trust Him. It's time to find your voice.

Kimberland Jackson

APRIL 5

DECLARATION: I decree and declare that through the lens of faith, we can see the evidence of His promises in our present reality.

AFFIRMATION: I am loved through all circumstances.

I remember the question as if it were yesterday. In a walk against inter-partner violence, my walking partner asked, "Who is part of your tribe?" I responded in reflective silence, and my mind is drawn to who was no longer a part of my tribe. At the time, I was still bleeding profusely from the fresh wound of family discord where the members of my family of origin and I were no longer speaking. Doubts covered me like a blanket. Perhaps I was not good enough, wise enough, brave enough. After all, I had been discarded. Didn't the Word promise that I was fearfully and wonderfully made? Didn't it speak of His love for me? My perspective of my reality did not reflect these truths.

I was in a battle with God to fulfill my desire through reconciliation now. Isn't settlement what He would desire? I shushed the voice that whispered, "In His time." My present circumstances quicken my heart with urgency. My husband and I were expecting. How could my heavenly Father want me to walk into this significant new chapter without my family? My walking partner that day pulled me from my fuming ruminations, "I hope you consider me part of your tribe." As those words sank in, my perspective widens. My tribe had been reformed since that painful split. Family members emerged from the shadows; new friendships formed; old friendships grew to a new level. My tribe was too many to count!

My heart fills with both hopes for healing and joy for the present. I've yielded to God's timing. My husband and I celebrated our son's third birthday with friends and family who have seen us through life's transitions. They've engulfed us in love, practical advice, and tangible service. We look forward to welcoming my son's new brother shortly. The trepidations that threaten the joy of our first pregnancy have evaporated. I no longer only focus on what I do not have, but gratefully see what I do.

Traumas impact our self-identity, our outlook, our very physiology. Sisters, God provides for all our needs. Exercise faith and the evidence will become a reality. Through the lens of faith, we can see that He already has the ball rolling to yield our desires. We are loved! Do you feel it? Broaden your perspective. Hold fast to God's truths. He is sovereign over all circumstances; across generations. The Lord provides for all our needs, including the desire of our hearts. Circumstances may whisper dark lies that seek to narrow our perspective. It may not appear in the form we envision. Do not be distracted by these limited views. Our Father's provisions are part of our present reality.

Andrea Phillips

I am using
my talents to
help others

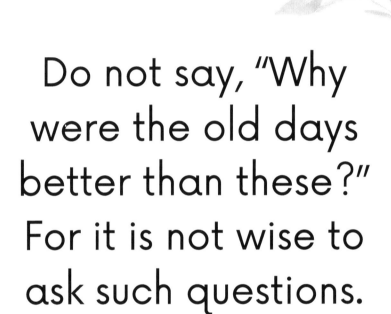

APRIL 7

Do not say, "Why were the old days better than these?" For it is not wise to ask such questions.

Ecclesiastes 7:10

APRIL 8

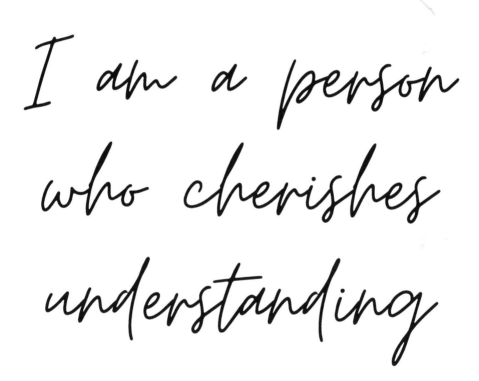

I am a person who cherishes understanding

I declare that I will guard my lips from evil speaking

APRIL 10

DECLARATION: I decree and declare that as a daughter of God, He completes me.

AFFIRMATION: I am fearfully and wonderfully made.

As a pre-teen, I was small and thin. I did not have many friends, and I stayed to myself. I remember we had picture day at school; my Mom told me to wear a particular skirt and blouse for pictures. I did not want to wear the outfit she chose because the top was laced with several ruffles down its front of the top and bottom of the sleeves. The skirt was frilly with lace in it. I did not like that outfit. As I walked to school that day, everything was normal. No one said anything to me about my outfit all day. I felt funny because I thought my outfit was old and outdated looking. Although I felt uneasy, I thought I had it made and proceeded home. During my walk home with my so-called "friends," someone said, "Girl, what are you wearing?" "Look at you, out here with your Laura Ingles outfit on!!" Laura Ingles was a character from a book and a television show named "Little House on the Prairie." I can admit it now, and the outfit did fit the accusation.

As I continued to walk home, more people started pointing and laughing at me and said, "Oh, look, it's Laura Ingles!" They taunted me almost the entire way home, laughing and pointing at me. I said to myself, "I will not let them see me cry! Just keep walking and get home." I was crushed and devastated on the inside. Walking home, I repeatedly commented to myself, "this will NEVER happen to me again. I will NEVER be laughed at about my clothes again." That drowned out the taunting for me. I did not know it then, but I made a soul vow. I vowed that I would never let anyone laugh at me again because of what I was wearing. This experience may seem small now, but then it was life-changing. But it was not a good change. The enemy sowed seeds in my life that day; seeds of insecurity, betrayal, resentment, and suspicion.

Since that day, I make it a point always to look my best. No matter what! Part of that is good, part of that is not. Image, it can be a struggle! Today, I am an avid shopper. I frequently shop with great satisfaction. It is my self-soothing mechanism. God is working with me about my image and shopping sprees. I am learning to depend solely on the Holy Spirit to teach me and fulfill me. It is a daily walk. In Christ, you must know, you are fearfully and wonderfully made. No matter what you face or go through, you are a daughter of God, and the Word says you are complete in Him.

May every fleshly vow made in our lives be cast down and destroyed by the power of the Holy Spirit. Whom the Son has set free is free indeed. We are COMPLETE and FREE in Him. God loves you and He wants you to stay free!

Kimberly Blackman

APRIL 11

Prayer List

Take the time to pray for others today and
put their names below

_____

_____

_____

_____

_____

_____

_____

_____

_____

_____

_____

_____

_____

_____

_____

_____

_____

Therefore everyone who hears these words of mine and puts them into practice is like a wise man who built his house on the rock.

Matthew 7:24

APRIL 13

DECLARATION: I decree and declare that I have the faith the size of a mustard seed, and with that faith, my prayers will move mountains!

AFFIRMATION: I am a survivor!

"Enough is enough!" Those were the last words I said to my husband as I walked out the door with our children on April 13, 2011, at 10:22 pm. I had enough with his mental abuse day after day. I had enough of walking on eggshells in constant fear of when he would physically hurt me. I had enough of acting like everything was ok when I was with family or friends. I had enough of his drinking night after night. I just had enough. I had a plan in place, but I honestly had no idea where the road ahead of me was going to take me. I knew that God was walking with me and my children, so I had faith that we were going to be just fine.

As I listened to a preacher on the radio one morning, he talked about the tiny mustard seed. He reminded me that Matthew 17:20 says if we "have faith the size of a mustard seed, we can move mountains!" That was a life-changing moment for me. God reminded me that no matter what I was going through, my faith was going to carry me through all the trials and tribulations.

I encountered some speed bumps along the way, but that little mustard seed helped me move every obstacle I faced. The morning the tires on my car were flat, I leaned on my faith and asked God to give me direction. I knew that the devil was trying to interfere with my kids getting to school and me to work.

I had to move mountains, and I did. I walked my kids to school. I was fortunate to be working at their school at the time, which relieved added stress. A friend was able to help me with the tires later that day. The moments I did not have enough money to buy extra groceries, I would thank God for the blessings I had.

An angel disguised as a friend would often appear at my front door with a bag of groceries or a complete dinner. I have been out of the abusive marriage for several years. God has called upon me to help other domestic violence victims learn how to live a life free from abuse. I am truly blessed.

God's constant love and abundant blessings are like a warm blanket on a cold day. You feel the warmth and comfort that touches your soul. That is how God's love feels all the time. You see, no matter what you are going through in life, you will get through it. God is always with us, and we must believe that with his love, we can surpass any obstacle. He will never let us down. God gets us through everything on His time and in His favor.

Nancy Gonzalez

APRIL 14

DECLARATION: I decree and declare that I will walk in freedom from shame and embrace vulnerability for God has forgiven me, and I can forgive myself also.

AFFIRMATION: I am able to walk with my head held high when convicted of wrongdoing and face the situation.

When I was nine years old, I spent that summer reading the book of Romans. I learned about forgiveness right before my world was about to change as I was about to learn that I was sexually abused and I would disclose the abuse immediately. I was able to forgive my cousin, and God allowed my family to heal. At a young age, I understood that God forgives me and how to strive not to make the same mistakes. But what that time in my life did not teach me is how to forgive myself and the shame that one feels that prevents you from forgiving yourself.

I was angry and ashamed because I fell prey to breaking several values that God instilled in me at an early age. I was not to have consensual sex before marriage. I was not to live with a man before marriage. I was not to enter into an ungodly marriage. I was not to become a statistic of divorce. I wish I could say that I did not see the signs before I entered the marriage, but God gave me glowing flags in the name of real transparency.

After going through therapy and talking with family and friends, I had to admit all the signs were there. From a best friend who flat out stated she did not think it was a good idea. To a father figure who woke up in the middle of the night and pinned a long heartfelt email. To a group of women who mentored me and spent a week trying to speak words into me. To the week before the wedding when my soon to be husband disappeared. To the moment right before walking down the aisle when my mother whispered: "You can change your mind." The signs were there. I was under the assumption that it was pride that kept me from canceling the wedding. I thought pride also kept me trapped in a marriage where I was psychologically abused. What I have learned in the last year is that it was more shame than pride.

If I admitted that I was wrong and that this marriage was wrong, then I would cease to belong with those I was connected to. None of my family and friends did or said anything to make me feel this way, and they supported me through this wrong decision. If God does not shame me for what I have done, who am I to shame myself for what I have done? We are women that can Live free of shame. God has forgiven us, and, therefore, we can forgive ourselves. Now open up and be vulnerable with your tribe. If you don't have a tribe, ask God to connect you with like-minded people who want to see you grow.

Dr. Shandra Davis

APRIL 15

Teach us to number our days, that we may gain a heart of wisdom.

Psalms 90:12

APRIL 16

I am no longer separated from God. I live in close union with him.

I produce fruit that brings great joy to God

APRIL 18

Encouragement

Take the time to encourage yourself today.
Write down your wins for the month!

_____
_____
_____
_____
_____
_____
_____
_____
_____
_____
_____
_____
_____
_____
_____
_____

APRIL 19

DECLARATION: I decree and declare that my faith shall is unshakeable.

AFFIRMATION: I am not barren, I am Fruitful.

I can remember it like it was just yesterday. It was Springtime in 2011 when I woke up from my mid-afternoon nap feeling rather strange. This strange feeling was not like any other feeling I had ever felt, but I was sure that with a bite to eat and a bit of relaxation, I would feel more like myself in a matter of time. With not much more thought of my feelings, I went for a quick bathroom break to discover my worst nightmare had come true. I had miscarried my six-week child! Thoughts and feelings of bitterness, shame, unworthiness, failure, and helplessness crept in my soul. How could the joy be taken away so quickly? No warning signs, no heads up, nothing! I had done everything that I felt was right; I took the prenatal vitamins, got enough rest, and took it easy at work, why then was this happening to me? Devastation, Emptiness, Anger, and Depression had become my new home. Weeks passed, and I found ways to cope by occupying my time, my thoughts, my emptiness with other things.

I attended small groups, picked up more shifts at work, spent more time out with friends, but nothing seemed to soothe the hurt and the pain that infected me on the inside. Finally, I gave in to my thoughts, acknowledged every trigger, and confronted all of my pain, and in my desperation, I wept! I wept for what I had lost. I wept for what I thought I had deserved. I wept in bitter sorrow to God. Mustering up all the faith I had left, I prayed one last prayer. Lord, at the right time, allow me to become a parent.

Within eight months, I began to breathe again, and I began to trust in the Lord again. I began to know with confidence that his plan was far better than any plan I had for myself and that His direction would eliminate my need for perfection. So, where am I today? Eight years later, I have a healthy seven-year-old handsome little boy. He is spunky, daring, fun, creative, and joyful. I finally understood how to stand on the firm foundation that was in me. Faith! To my surprise, my faith, tears, and pain turned into my favorite blessing of all time. Your faith will produce your blessings, your miracles, your joy, your happiness. Stand in Faith!

We stand on faith in hard times, in times of loss, in times of heartache, in times of pain and discomfort. In times of unexpected circumstances, stand on faith and faith alone! Your faith to know it will get better when it does not seem to look how you imagined it should. It is your faith that will sustain you in every season!

Shawntrel Pierre

APRIL 20

DECLARATION: I decree and declare that the whole me is greater than the holes that were in me.

AFFIRMATION: I am whole and worth the wait.

"You are a great and beautiful woman, but I just do not see myself being with you for the rest of my life." Those are the words that pierced my heart in 2011. I wish I could say my mantra was "Well, I am not gon' cry, I am not gon' cry, I am not gon' shed no tears," as Mary J. Blige would say. However, that's not my testimony. I cried many tears because I was devastated. He pursued me and I soon learned he was unavailable. Why couldn't I cut him off when I learned of his unavailability in 2009? I was lonely and had created a soul tie. Loneliness was such a deep hole that I gave away pieces of myself trying to keep someone who was never mine. I believed I was not worth any man waiting for, so I compromised my commitment to God, personal standards, and was no longer practicing what I was preaching.

Have you ever been there? Filled with holes that got deeper when you compromised and lowered your standards? You had all the information you needed upfront that showed you a "DEAD END" was ahead. If this is your current situation, God says return to Him and let go of what or who you think you have. After those words, as mentioned earlier that pierced my heart, God gave me hope when He penetrated my soul with these words: "Now you can be available for the person I have for you." God took me through a healing process that revealed a pattern of involvement with unavailable men and expecting relationships to fill holes that only God can. I then began to believe that if God had someone for me, that person would be willing to wait for me. I did not know when God would do it, but I knew I would be whole, and I would be worth the wait.

In 2013, when I was content in my singleness, God brought me the man I am privileged to call my husband today. Not only was I whole and worth his wait, but he was also worth my wait! It was finally my time to begin service as a wife, specifically to who God gave me. Sis, who God gives you and gives you to will be strategic, purposeful, and timely. Trust that God will grace you both to wait on each other. In the meantime, focus on returning to God so your healing process can begin. Between a therapist, accountability partner(s), a legit prayer life, and deliverance in some instances, God will make you whole. What God did for me, He will do for you: Hear your cry. Lift you out of a horrible pit. Set your feet on a rock, and put a new song in your mouth that'll cause others to trust Him (Psalm 40:1-3). We shall decree and declare, together, that the whole us is greater than the holes that were in us!

Meoshia Wilson

APRIL 21

Through the energy of Christ working powerfully in me, I teach others His truths.

Colossians 1:29

I am whole
in my spirit,
soul, and
body

APRIL 23

DECLARATION: I decree and declare that the pain I experienced upon the loss and burial of my stillborn child was not in vain.

AFFIRMATION: I am resilient and more durable than I could have ever imagined; God does not make mistakes.

I became pregnant with our third child, DeJay, in August of 2017, one month after marrying my lifelong sweetheart. He was due to be our last, but the first that we would welcome into our marriage union, along with his eight-year-old brother and three-year-old sister. But God had other plans. It was a Friday morning in February of 2018 when my nurse instructed us to go to the hospital to have my baby checked because his movement had decreased. I had experienced that before with my firstborn, so I mentally prepared myself to deliver Dejay at 28 weeks also. However, about 30 minutes after checking into labor and delivery, the nurse didn't come into the room to say I was delivering early, she came in to say that my precious baby DeJay's heart had stopped.

I was NOT prepared for that diagnosis and would have never guessed it in my wildest nightmare or imagination. The following twelve hours of labor to birth my lifeless baby was so heartbreaking. I kept praying that they had made a mistake, but they hadn't. I had birthed him, but there was still no life in his perfect little body. I spent two nights in the hospital, and the day I was released to go home, I went straight for a bottle of vodka and drank until I could barely function. I cried, drifted in and out of sleep, drank, and cried some more; I yelled, cursed, and found myself angry at God for taking my baby.

I was in a state of complete darkness and anger during the first two weeks after we buried him, and I honestly felt like letting go of my own life so I could join him because in my mind, I had failed as a woman, mother, and wife. I should have known something was wrong, but didn't. No one did. The doctor never found nor confirmed the cause of death. It was indeed the lowest point and worst pain that I had ever experienced in my life, but God was with me throughout the process. He sent many different women to share their stories of stillbirth and showed me that I was stronger in Him than I had ever imagined. I grew closer to my husband and other children, and three months after losing our baby, God blessed us with baby number four, Dre, due in the same month as baby DeJay. Look at God!

What I came to realize was that there was/is power in being resilient and not giving up. I'm healthier because of that life-altering experience, and since then, I have helped other women to get through similar experiences. Despite the immense pain and struggle of this world, we must come to know that things happen to and for us that may stretch, bruise, hurt, and cause us to nearly break, but if we hang on with all our might and being, we become resilient, one step and one day at a time.

Princess Johnson

APRIL 24

I have been saved, not by works, but grace, so that I might do good works.

Ephesians 2:9-10

My mind is full of brilliant ideas.

I am headed in the right direction.

APRIL 27

DECLARATION: I decree and declare that by the power of God invested in me, everyone around me shall know that they matter to God!

AFFIRMATION: I am undeniable, unstoppable, and amazing!

Before I knew or even understood the existence or essence of me. My shame, insecurities, and lack of self-confidence employed my acceptance of the lesser of "self & love" as oppose to the greater! As I looked through the glass dimly of the world, relationships, and friendships, I only saw my low self-esteem, my insecurities, my need for acceptance and others' opinions. I allowed them to handle and break the spirit of me. Which all turned out to be a lie and an understatement to my identity. It was out of the rubble of my brokenness, and in the rescue of God's grace, I learned my true identity. I know that you are fearfully and wonderfully made. Shaped in purpose and destiny, you were created in the image and likeness of the creator, full of divine strength and glory! I learned that in our weakness, it is then, in God, that we are strong. I wrestled with acceptance and a sense of belonging for a large part of my life. Only to learn that I was already accepted in the beloved of God! He loved me to wholeness and good health. When He created us, He did so in the image and likeness of His divine being.

Clothed and housed us in a wrapping of his choosing. The essence, the beauty, and the power of you, your presence, your voice, and yes, your silence is resounding. And when he created us, He (God) stepped back, looked us over, smiled, and said, oh yes, it is very good! You see, we belong; we've always belonged, and it was God who deemed it so! We were always meant to be. The power, the strength, and the resilience of you speak volumes. What are you saying? Whatever it is, it has a rippling effect and know this; they both (it and you) matter. They are speaking to someone, delivering someone, strengthening someone, empowering someone, and mending broken pieces and will catapult someone into their awesome, great, and powerful selves. And, put them on the pathway to the healing of their heart and soul. I became accustomed to being let down, overlooked, and counted out that I took on and subconsciously accepted that view of me and deemed myself unworthy. Be mindful of what you're feeding your inner being. How do you nourish your soul? The power of you is a force to be reckoned with. The greatest gift unto man is love!

Shower yourself with and soak in it, dine with it and lavish yourself in it. You are well deserving and well worthy of love! For we can only love others as we love ourselves! May you be empowered and may you soar in life, purpose, and destiny on the strength, power, and resilience of you! You are the sum total of whom God has created you to be, and of whom you believe! And let nothing or no one rob you of that!

Sharon Graves

When I call out to
God He answers me.
He tells me things I
wouldn't know
otherwise.

Jeremiah 33:3

APRIL 29

DECLARATION: I decree and declare that I will not allow unforgiveness to take root in my heart, causing family division.

AFFIRMATION: I am forgiven, healed, and free.

Has there ever been a time in your life when you felt hurt by a parent? In the past, I have experienced challenges with my mother. Growing up, my mother tried her her best to balance it all while battling with her past trauma and hurts, and it would spill into our mother-daughter relationship. The injury planted a seed of blame, criticism, judgment, anger, and resentment in my heart towards my mother. I lost time because I wore a mask and tried to handle everything through my works apart from God. Internally my heart was filled with anger and frustration battling internal issues that affected my relationships; I began to withdraw.

My grandmother was my second parent; she was very nurturing and taught me all about God. She was gentle despite all the trauma she had endured in life, and she always told me to forgive others, and to keep a clean heart, I can still hear her singing the song in my head. In November of 2018, my grandmother passed away, a couple of weeks later, my grandmother came to me in a dream, and she told me two things, one of them was to love my mother. I love her, but my mother was tough to deal with, and I didn't do an excellent job of hiding it. It was May 2020, and I had spent the last two years praying for healing for myself and my mother. I joined an online bible study, and the topic was the Parable of talents and forgiveness. After reflection, God began to speak into my heart. I felt lighter and my spirit from the pit of my stomach, after repentance and apologies, I was free.

Something powerful happens to us when we forgive others and ourselves. When we forgive, it heals us, and where there was death, new life comes to all aspects of our life. When we forgive others as God instructs us, we are free from manipulation as we truly put others in His hands. We can love better and love unconditionally. We are no longer are offended by every little comment. We practice grace and humility in our life. We become gentle and are less critical of ourselves and others. We will see that we are more open to give and receive love. We can trust other people and pour into them even if they can't return the love. We all have been hurt and have struggled, but when we forgive, we are free, and our hearts are healed and made pure. That is the way God wants us to live and the only way we can be vessels of life.

Angelica LaGuerre

Because I place my
hope in the Lord my
strength is renewed.

Isaiah 40:31

May

MAY 1

Goal Setting

Use today to set your goals for the year.
Be clear and specific with what you want to achieve.
Break the goal down into steps.
All the best in achieving your goals this year!

_____

_____

_____

_____

_____

_____

_____

_____

_____

_____

_____

_____

_____

_____

_____

MAY 2

I am unique

I am walking
in peace

Because I obey Jesus I remain in his love.

John 15:10

MAY 5

DECLARATION: I decree and declare that God's plans for me are good and not evil.

AFFIRMATION: I am healed, to show forth the power and faithfulness of God.

On 5/5/5 (5 is the number of grace), I worked in corporate America at my desk, minding my own business when my supervisor took me from my desk, put me in his car, and took me to the ER. Once at the ER, a gentleman asked to speak with me (I later found out he was the coroner), so we went into a nearby office. The gentleman told me, "There's been an accident, and your daughter didn't make it." When he said those words, my whole world shattered! I lost it! All I know is that the papers on that desk were now all over the room, the computer from the desk was now on the floor, and I think I beat that poor coroner black and blue! I dropped my baby girl off at daycare that morning, and now this man is telling me my baby girl is gone! My 4-year-old daughter, Destinee Faith, died in a car accident while in the car with the childcare provider.

There were five other children in the car, the childcare provider, and her husband. No one was injured or hurt, except my daughter Destinee. Immediately in the ER, The Holy Spirit instructed me to forgive the childcare provider. I went to her in the ER and sincerely told her I forgive her. I can tell you that I was devastated, heartbroken, crushed, and angry, but that does not even begin to convey the pain that I felt. My spirit shattered. There were days I couldn't even speak, cry, or pray. All I could do is moan. Today I am healed, whole, full of love, and joy. God has given me beauty for ashes; He has given me the oil of joy for mourning. We must have the heart to forgive those that have hurt us. Forgiveness attracts God! We have to ask and allow the Holy Spirit to move on our hearts and help us forgive the person that hurt us, and if necessary, we have to forgive ourselves.

We have to know that regardless of what we go through, God is with us and He loves us. We must speak His word and scriptures out loud. Scriptures like Jeremiah 29:11, "His plans are good for you and not evil, to give you a hope and a future." We should speak God's word out loud so we can hear ourselves saying it. Faith comes by hearing. The more we listen to ourselves saying it, the deeper it will get rooted in our spirit. I want to encourage you, if there are days that you truly, honestly, can't muster up the strength to speak back His word, the Holy Spirit will take your moan before the Father and worship Him with it. So, you are still covered!

Theresa Faith Adams

I am confident that my God meets all my needs.

MAY 7

DECLARATION: I decree and declare that God has a plan for my life to prosper and win!

AFFIRMATION: I am drawing upon, the strength, and courage of God to step out of my circumstances.

A word of encouragement to someone: Don't give up, keep moving forward One day I woke up and was unable to get out of bed and move into my activities of the day.   I realized my inability to get out of bed was because I was overwhelmed emotionally, overworked, and burned out, exhausted, and stagnated.   I experienced these emotions because I was BROKEN. I was living up to the expectations of others. I lost a sense of myself, who was I becoming? To address the root cause of my brokenness, I embarked on a journey. I moved from a place where I was highly connected to a network of people to a place where I only knew one person.

The purpose and the relocation were for me to self-assess, and recalibrate the direction of my life. After the honeymoon phase, my journey started with many trails, and moments I did not know what my next steps were going to be. Seven months into my relocation, Due to unforeseen circumstances, I found myself being homeless. During this time, all I had were these words from Our Father. Seek ye first the Kingdom of God and His righteousness and all things will be added unto you. Cast your cares on me because I care for you. I have perfected EVERYTHING that concerns YOU!

Our Father has kept me even when others, including myself, have left me disappointed. There were many days on my journey that I questioned my purpose. I was walking through the fire. However, the more I confessed the three scriptures, and rest knowing and trusting, He is my provider. I began to see God's hand in my situation. He placed people in my path who offered me a place to stay, who shared a word of encouragement. Who prayed with me, who interceded on my behalf. God has expanded my territory, and network and has shown me that I can operate in His purpose anywhere and has an extended system. I no longer have my expectations in people but my Father.

I have experienced uncertainty, but through my Father's strength, I found the courage to keep moving despite the challenges I was facing. We give all honor and praise to you, Father, for Your LOVE and GRACE upon our lives provides us with the power to withstand any trial or tribulation. We are leaving the past in the past, never looking or turning back. In every battle that we face, we put on God's full armor to fight the good fight of faith.

We put our trust in you, Father, because you love us, and you will not leave us stranded in the wilderness nor forsake us.

Angelette Verdena-King

I place my hope in God

MAY 10

DECLARATION: I decree and declare that God can turn my bad into good; no matter what I've been through in life.

AFFIRMATION: I am whole because I have found my true identity in Christ Jesus.

I have overcome past trauma by allowing God to make me whole again. As a young child, I suffered from sexual abuse. At the age of eight, I began being sexually abused by a family member. In 1984, at the age of 14, the sexual abuse by my biological father began. As a result, I conceived a son who was born in 1989. Before the abuse, I was indeed a daddy's girl. He was the one person I trusted and loved more than anything. I felt like he failed me miserably. My innocence was violently ripped away. The downward spiral began. I lost my self-worth and ability to trust others. My love and admiration soon turned into fear, hatred, and disgust. For over 25 years, I kept the secret and suppressed the trauma. At an early age, I was taught, "what goes on in my house stays in my house." I was deadly afraid of my father and wouldn't dare tell a soul. I never felt like I had a voice, and besides, who would believe me? My father was held in high regard and loved by many.

In 2016, God put it on my heart to tell my story. I could no longer suppress and keep the "family secret." So, I was obedient to the Spirit. I came out and talked about the sexual abuse by my father. I received a variety of responses from family and friends. But the family members that disowned me and said I was lying hurt the most. The abuse left me feeling insecure and worthless. I never felt like I was good enough and always longed for love and acceptance. Those feelings carried over into my adulthood and had an adverse effect on all of my relationships. Can you relate to feeling ashamed, insecure, worthless, not good enough, or needing to feel accepted? I didn't realize how broken I was until I began to notice that all my relationships were failing. I was the problem. I had a victim mentality. During self-reflection, I realized I rarely took responsibility for my actions. I became depressed and wanted to give up on life. It was time to make a change, so I began Christian counseling.

My counselor taught me how to replace negative thoughts with God's promises. I realized the importance of forgiving my father. Forgiveness is the key to freedom. It enables you to take back your power and break the chains of bondage. You must break any silence to heal the pain. God will turn Satan's bad intentions into good. God can turn any pain into purpose. You don't have to feel ashamed or fearful. Break the bondage of feeling insecure, worthless, and unloved. Face challenges head-on because what we have endured in the past does not determine our future. God can turn any situation into good!

Latarsha Haughton

MAY 11

Encouragement

Take the time to encourage yourself today. Write down your wins for the month!

_____
_____
_____
_____
_____
_____
_____
_____
_____
_____
_____
_____
_____
_____
_____
_____
_____

MAY 12

DECLARATION: I decree and declare that I am anointed to finish this race!

AFFIRMATION: I am anointed to continue!

Have people ever told you, you don't look like what you've been through? I've heard this many times, and I always credit the anointing of God as my life preserver. Like you, I have come through many traumas, trials, and tragedies in my life. But I've grown to adopt the thinking of Maya Angelou when she said, "you cannot control all the events that happen to you, but you can decide not to be reduced by them."
One of the hardest seasons to live through was when I gave my twin daughters up for adoption. I was 26 years old, pregnant, and homeless because of poor choices. I hadn't told my family about the rape and sexual abuse I suffered when I was younger. Therefore, they didn't understand that my poor behavior flowed from an unattended festering wound. So, their support was inadequate. I was traumatized and hopeless from carrying the weight of shame and guilt for over a decade.

I already had two sons that were paying for my shame. I didn't want these children to pay as well. They deserved a better life, and I believed that life was without me - the source of their shame. Have you ever been in a place of darkness and despair, without vision or hope for the next day? How did you escape that place? My miracle did not come overnight. What did immediately occur after the twins were born was an "opportunity" for a new career. This gave me a glimmer of hope and vision for a different future and started me on the path to my miracle. As years passed, I developed a relationship with God and confided in my family. My wounds were tended by my family and healed by God's words. Today, after years of miraculous life-shifting words, faith decisions, and God-orchestrated events, I can happily testify that my daughters and I know each other, love each other and see each other as often as we desire.

I received my miracle! I've learned many lessons throughout my life, but the key is that words frame our lives. The first word of affirmation the Lord spoke in my spirit will always resonate with me, "You are anointed to continue!" God knew I was scared and wanted me to know that no matter what I faced, he already anointed me for it, and I was to continue living full-out no matter what! The next affirmation came a few years later to secure my destiny. He encouraged me, saying, "You are anointed to finish and finish well!" And finish well, I shall!

I encourage you today with these three words, "Just don't die!" I promise you, if you keep living and loving and believing beyond this moment, you will wake up one day, and you will have outlived the shame, pain, or trauma that you feel today. I am evidence! Declare with me today, "I am anointed to continue, I am built to last, and I have the right to be here!"

Marguerite Isaac

MAY 13

DECLARATION: I decree and declare that I am a chiropractor in the spirit of God; my misalignment changed my purpose.

AFFIRMATION: I am healed and aligned because of God's touch.

The date was January 14, 2020, when I maneuvered toward my uncertainty with troubling emotions. Courtroom #62 was busy, and the caseload was hectic for the state attorney. Overwhelmed by the chaos in courtroom #62 caused a shift to another Judge, and suddenly my heart sank into despair. Then the mix of emotions went from elated to confused to embarrassment. As I looked over to the side of the courtroom at my family, my spine and mind felt unaligned. The misalignment of emotions pierced my soul and made my spirit feel lethargic. "Chiropractic," a holistic alternative that removes the subluxation of interference, encased my thoughts. I had adjusted many patients over the years, which permitted me to remove interference so that the body could heal and function as God intended. The purpose of innate, as defined in many dictionaries, is an inborn or natural state of wellness. Suddenly, my emotions were in a state of subluxation due to a misalignment of pain and interference. My heart was overshadowed with grief as the ruling was announced. "Not guilty," two words that haunted me as I watched eight jurors determine my fate January 14 in courtroom #62. The evidence of blackened bruises was questionable based on a prior veteran status created an enraged emotion.

The toxic relationship that controlled my life was coming to an end; my health was failing, the average blood sugar is 70-100, and mine was 580 fasting because of the stress. My emotions in a catabolic state of brokenness left me in a state of vulnerability and disease. The blow to my temporal skull was felt with anger, then the knot that formed in my neck from the fist, had me spinning uncontrollably. All I could do was look up towards heaven and ask the question, "why me?". I felt the kicks with intense pain as his foot penetrated my ribs. Every breath recreated a pain index that was unbearable, over and over again. I found myself begging for relief while questioning his intentions. The human saliva that lubricated my face was a harsh reality that caused my self-esteem to sink to its lowest point. My thought process went to prayer and revenge and suddenly reasoning. God answered my prayers, delivered me, even when the case ruling was "not guilty".

Chiropractors work with subtle substances of the soul to release an imprisoned impulse. The spirit of God was felt within my soul, and continued the flow within my nervous system and was innate to sustain survival. My state of mind propelled me to a higher power that exists that was greater than a human emotional roller coaster presented in the physical realm. God is waiting to realign your trouble in the spirit. It doesn't matter what you are facing or what you are dealing with in your life. You were created with all of the tools necessary to get back in alignment. All it takes is just one touch from God!

Dr. Sonja Brookins

MAY 14

DECLARATION: I decree and declare that my story is not yet over. I know that despite the trials and tribulations, my story ends in victory.

AFFIRMATION: I am resilient. God's favor is always with me, he has never left my side.

As I look at this journey called life and I think of all that I have had to endure. I continue to reflect deeply on my life's journey and I quickly realize that I have more to be thankful for than ever. I look back at a time where I felt all was lost and hopeless. After separating from my now ex-husband, I moved to Massachusetts in 2010 per my aunt's suggestion. I had decided I needed a fresh start and to work on things from afar. I needed consistency and I got tired of the roller coaster ride, the broken promises, and the short-term change.

Memorial day 2011, my ex-husband decided to make a surprise visit. We went for a walk around Boston, and suddenly his mood changed; my older and young cousins who we were spending time with me looked at me puzzled. I was filled with disappointment; I thought to myself "there he goes again". While trying to figure out what was wrong, it escalated into an argument. I then decided that it was over for good. Upon realizing that I was serious and that there was no turning back, things spiraled out of control. Next thing I recall is being punched and thrown out of my car. I saw the rear lights abruptly come towards me and I was run over and left on the side of the street like a piece of garbage.

After coming from the hospital the following day and realizing that the support I thought I had from the family was no longer there, I found myself pregnant, in a state that was unknown to me. I ended up in a Domestic Violence shelter, alone, broken, lost, and bitter. My faith shattered, I felt defeated and wished for death. I've always felt as if my life has been a battle against the devil; I was ready to surrender and let him win, after all, my faith was not like that of Job. My anger blinded me from seeing that my child was a victim too, and I contemplated the comments of "get an abortion before it's too late" and "you can always give it up for abortion." These thoughts reverberated through my mind. Terrified and helpless, I cried out to God and asked him to please save my child, and if he did, I would fight through this depression, the suicidal idealizations and strive to be the best mother I can be. The mother my child needs me to be and God heard my plea.

All of our journeys follow a different path where we find ourselves at different stages. Just because you are not there yet, does not mean that your story is over. One or a few bad chapters does not define your whole story. My story is not yet over. I know that despite the trials and tribulations, my story ends in victory because I am resilient. God's favor will always be with you. You are fearfully and wonderfully made. You are the daughter of the King, the great I Am.

Nahomie Prophete

I am
becoming a
better version
of myself
everyday

I love who I am right now because I am exactly where God needs me to be

LORD my God, I called to you for help, and you healed me.

Psalm 30:2

MAY 18

DECLARATION: I decree and declare that it doesn't matter who rejects me, for I am loved completely, favored, and fully accepted in God's Beloved.

AFFIRMATION: I am loveable, valuable, and worthy of pure unconditional love.

Am I good enough? How could you walk away from me? What did I do, at the age of 8 years old, to make you leave me? You said you would always be my dad, but you left me anyway. Yes, the story is complicated, but what did I do to deserve the hurt and disappointment? I must not be loveable or even worthy of his love, were all thoughts that would run through my mind. My dad wasn't the only one who rejected me and eventually abandoned me. It was a beautiful love story, so it seemed. I met him at the age of 14 and was with him for 26 years (married for 20). We know that marriages are never perfect and have ups and downs, but eventually, decisions were made that ended up being the best for both of us. Could you imagine, going through even more rejection from your very own husband? Maybe the tragedy in this entire story is that some of you can, and it's all too familiar.

Too numerous are the stories of "daddy issues," infidelity, or even just not feeling wanted, pushed away – REJECTED by men either by birth or marriage, vowed to love us forever. I did all that I could do to make him love me; I turned myself inside out. I would ask my husband, "What do you want me to change? I will do it, tell me." I was a perfectionist, an overachiever to the core. What was I trying to prove? Just maybe, I will be good enough for him to stay true to me and love me for me.

In March 2012, there was yet another incident of infidelity, and that was the final straw! The pain and agony of the betrayal cut me to my very core, but this time was not like
before. I stood up for myself and finally said no more! I asked him to leave. That was my turning point. He decided that he didn't want to hurt me anymore and filed for the divorce. The divorce was final in 2013, and I was finally set free!

One thing, this journey taught me was how to forgive. Over the years, I was able to release the pain of my dad and my ex-husband's rejection and abandonment through many tears, prayers, and counseling. I am not a victim of rejection and divorce, I am a victor over rejection and divorce, with another opportunity to be loved unconditionally, the way God intended. When we are rejected by our husbands, relatives, and friends, we often don't understand what we have done to deserve this treatment. We must always remember and be encouraged, "It's not really rejection, but we are under love's protection and entirely accepted in the beloved.

Dr Tylisha Johnson

MAY 19

I am patient

I hold my head high because I am everything that God says I am!

Come to me, all you who are weary and burdened, and I will give you rest.

Matthew 11:28

MAY 22

DECLARATION: I decree and declare that other women and I will understand self-care and realize that it's fundamental to living a happier and healthier life.

AFFIRMATION: I am committed to living my life with passion and with purpose.

Life is not always easy, but there have never been any guarantees that it would be. We all have experienced life challenges in various forms. A primary life challenge for me started in August of 2005 when I realized that I was not taking very good care of myself. I was taking care of everyone in my family except for me. I paid very little attention to my own needs and wants, which left me bitter, frustrated, and with low self-esteem. I was in a state of despair and was struggling to find my purpose. I was blaming everyone else for my problems, but the truth is that I was comfortable and didn't know how to navigate out of the situation.

One summer, I attended a seminar in Atlanta, Georgia, when I heard the speaker telling my exact story; of putting everyone else's needs ahead of hers. She overcame this dilemma through positive thinking and realizing that her needs and wants were essential too. After listening to her, I knew something had to change. This initiated my self-care journey. I decided to show up for myself every day and began to do some of the things that made me happy. I started to include my needs and wants on my daily "things-to-do list." My situation began to change as I began practicing self-care and positive thinking. I discovered that if I invaded my thoughts with positive affirmations, I could win the battle of negative thinking.

If we are struggling with positive thoughts of ourselves, we must think about positive things and situations we want to see in our lives and repeat them to ourselves throughout the day. We should go to our bible and find out what the word of God says about us. After locating the positive affirmations, declare them out loud, and often, that is what I did. I wrote them down and stated them repeatedly until I started to see change. I declared these affirmations with confidence. I declared and verbalized them until I believed them. Remember, affirmations have to be said more than once.

We can use affirmations to break all the barriers of negative thinking. There is so much power in the spoken word. When we use words to affirm, uplift, and motivate, the impact can be life changing. I know that affirmations are a valuable tool in my arsenal of self-care. Taking better care of myself allowed me to be the author and entrepreneur that I am today. When we take better care of ourselves, we become better mothers, better wives, better sisters, and better friends; we also become better servants of God.

Sheila Green

MAY 23

DECLARATION: I decree and declare that I am what God says I am, and I can do what He says I can do.

AFFIRMATION: I am called to do a mighty work, and God has equipped me to complete it.

I recall the season I was in before becoming licensed as a mental health provider. I had my doctorate and was frustrated that the plan I had to finish school with my license had not panned out. Throughout my schooling, I was overwhelmed. I always excelled in school, but I did not do well in my first year of the program. After seeking some assistance, I was diagnosed with Attention Deficit Hyperactivity Disorder at 29 years of age. I still remember the faculty suggesting that I rethink my enrollment and consider dropping the program. I was overworked. Responsible for leading an ill-prepared yet tenured staff, I was on a sinking ship, which would eventually lead to a very public exit from that organization for all of us. I was over-committed. My role as wife, mom, and ministry leader regularly threatened my commitment to finish school on time. The most limiting of all was the fact that I was over myself! I had a good plan, but the plan did not include preparing for my state exam. I was not faring well on my simulated practice tests. Frankly, I was failing the practice tests. I could not afford to fail the actual test. It was expensive, and I was laid off with no job opportunities in sight.

Why did I allow myself to become so distracted? I needed to pass the required state exam to become licensed, and I was fighting discouragement. Everything seemed to be out of sync. I needed to pass the exam so I could recover financially. Determined not to get lost in a pool of pity, I decided to pull it together. I stretched myself spiritually. I sought the Scripture for an anchor. I knew it was important to regroup. I knew God was responsible for every victory I ever had. I knew that everything challenging me in that season had to work for my good, according to the word of God. So, it was time for me to agree with the word of God. God's name had to be elevated above the circumstances surrounding me. Who was I to disagree with the One who never fails? His word had to be higher than my discouragement. The word of God started my journey, and it had to finish the job. I passed my test on the first try! This is true for you too! God has created us in His image.

We are called to create and develop in the earth. We are commanded to be fruitful, multiply, replenish, and dominate in this earth. Will you let God's word rise in your heart today? You are in the driver's seat. Search out what He says about you and then say it. God's word in our mouths is just as powerful!

Dr. Shnai Simmons

I speak only
with love

There is
power in my
tongue

But I will restore you
to health and heal
your wounds,
declares the LORD

Jeremiah 30:17

MAY 27

DECLARATION: I decree and declare that no matter where I am and what season is occurring, God, our Father, is always covering and protecting.

AFFIRMATION: I am covered by my faithful Father, and His divine interventions are for our protection.

I have had many "close calls" before, but March 23rd, 2018, was a traumatizing event and one that if it did not happen to me and if I did not have the pictures to prove it, I would not have believed it myself. That day started pretty typically, except that my husband was out of town visiting family, and I had taken a half-day off from work to study for an essential upcoming examination. Little did I know that that day would then turn into divine intervention.

When I arrived home that early afternoon, my dog was very anxious for me to take him outside. I walked into the bedroom, changed my shoes quickly, and headed out. Our walk was interestingly longer than usual, but I thought it was due to my husband's absence, realizing later that this was due to God's interference. After we completed our walk, I opened the front door, released Dieppe from his leash, and changed clothes to prepare for study mode.

As I walked down my hallway headed to my office, I suddenly observed a hole in my hallway wall that I did not see before. I called my husband instantly to video chat and inquired if he noticed the hole in the wall before he left. He immediately said no and that I should report it to the management office. I then started wondering what could have caused this hole. Perplexed, I walked to the management office, which was closed until Monday, so I followed up with email correspondence with a photo attached. The weekend was a bit unsettling as I waited for additional answers, and I realized that when I left to take my dog for a walk, that is when the incident occurred.

When Monday approached, I made my way to the front office, and management accompanied me to my condominium, confirming what I had begun to become suspicious of. A bullet had created that hole, and I just missed the event within seconds thanks to my insistent dog. After management and police investigations, I was made aware that my neighbor's AR-15 rifle had misfired during handling in his condominium, which penetrated four walls, my husband's wardrobe, and eventually lodged into the master closets door frame. The officer who was first on the scene noted that I was "very blessed" to have missed the entire event, and all I could do was nod in agreement. As I walked back into my living room, I began to acknowledge His presence. I now realize that His unmerited favor is not only guiding and providing but covering and protecting. Not only is God doing that for me, but He is also doing that for you!

Natalie Ragland

MAY 28

I do not have
to do it all

I am not going to compare myself to others

And my God will meet all your needs according to the riches of his glory in Christ Jesus.

Philippians 4:19

MAY 31

Encouragement

Take the time to encourage yourself today. Write down
your wins for the month!

_____

_____

_____

_____

_____

_____

_____

_____

_____

_____

_____

_____

_____

June

JUNE 1

Goal Setting

Use today to set your goals for the year.
Be clear and specific with what you want to achieve.
Break the goal down into steps.
All the best in achieving your goals this year!

_____

_____

_____

_____

_____

_____

_____

_____

_____

_____

_____

_____

_____

_____

_____

JUNE 2

DECLARATION: I decree and declare that that I am FREE from pain, rejection, isolation, ridicule, and verbal abuse.

AFFIRMATION: I am abiding in His presence where I receive His love, comfort, power, and strength to fulfill my purpose.

Trauma seemed to be at the center of my life in my formative years, which resulted in a little girl feeling lost, voiceless, and broken. I WAS DIFFERENT! It started in my beginnings; I was born three months premature weighing in at 2 lbs. 4 oz. As I began to learn how to walk as a toddler, the doctor diagnosed me with cerebral palsy. In elementary school, I quickly learned that other children were not accepting of people with different abilities. I was called cripple by other children because I walked with a limp. Day after day, I was scorn, harassed, mocked, and laughed at, my voice became silenced. As a way to cope, I became invisible. I would be present in the classroom but absent from the activities and the lessons of the day. I accepted the mockery because I suffered verbal abuse at home. Unfortunately, I thought this was normal. No one knew the pain; I was enduring because no one was listening. There was no ear to hear, no heart to extend or express compassion or empathy. Drugs and alcohol consumed the adults in my world. They, too, were invisible, voiceless, and suffering pain from their wounds. The spirit of fear had run its course in my life. I believed the lie that something was wrong with me; the pain was unbearable. At 17 years old, I was underperforming and asked to leave high school to attend an alternative high school. I just wanted OUT!

Early on, through all the torment of people calling me cripple. I developed a relationship with our Comforter, Counselor, Helper, Intercessor, Advocate, Strengthener, and Standby, the Holy Spirit. He had an ear to hear, my concerns. He had a heart to express His compassion and empathy through His Word. Rest assured, what the enemy meant for evil, to stop our purpose; God has worked it out for our good. We embrace your love Father, your love has cast out the spirit of fear, the spirit of self-doubt, the spirit of failure and quitting, the spirit of low self- esteem, the spirit lack and insufficiency, the spirit of insecurity, and lack of self-confidence, the spirit of rejection, the spirit of self-hatred, and hatred from others. We should accept and trust in God's ways and love for us. We must know that God has plans for our lives and plans to prosper us and not harm us.

His plans provide us with hope and a future, exceedingly, abundantly above anything we can think or ask. We must stand in our truth of who Our Heavenly Father called us to be. We are perfectly and wonderfully made. Know that you were created in His image and likeness. You are chosen, you are royalty, and you are peculiar on purpose. Our Father has called us out of the darkness into His marvelous light. For we are all individually different, made with unique talents, gifts, and abilities. We are His Masterpiece. We are the original people. Father, we let nothing separate us from the POWER of Your LOVE.

Angelette Verdena-King

I am grateful
to wake up
each day

Your gift must be submitted to God!

I am not going to hold onto what God is ripping apart

JUNE 6

DECLARATION: I decree and declare that I am free from the shackles of living a life trying to prove my fleshly worth.

AFFIRMATION: I am more than enough, and I am made In His image to fulfill His purpose!

I never realized how hard it was to love my neighbor as I loved myself. I found that I loved people the way I loved myself, and newsflash, I struggled with loving myself. Like so many other women, I am and have been very critical of me. I never thought that I was enough and struggled with a lack of self-esteem and self -validation. I have since learned that my lack of tolerance for myself and desire to "prove" was a reflection of how I believed the world saw me, and I had begun to see myself through those same eyes. Molded by rejection, life hurts, the mistakes I had made, and countless imperfections. I don't know exactly when it started, but I do remember when it became so clear that I was, in essence, unworthy. It was during my journey to become a Physical Therapist. It was my second semester in the undergraduate program, and I struggled to keep up all year. I found myself for the first time failing in school. I still remember the words from the Dean during my academic counseling session, "you are the type of student that would go on to embarrass the entire University!" Those words sunk so deep within me that even though I would later go on and complete my degree, I would remain haunted by that jarring failure. I thought that everyone knew I was a failure and could instantly tell the moment they looked at me. That thought consumed me and drove me to perfection.

I was so critical of myself that I became critical of the ones I loved. My "neighbors" had to bear the brunt of my judgments and corrections. I found myself demanding perfection, harsh with criticisms, unrelenting, unforgiving, and unyielding. The haunting failures, fears of rejection, and self-scathing criticism in all aspects of my life were blinded by the notion of what I was convinced that everyone else could see. I fought to prove something rather than focusing on improving something. When we look at ourselves through a jaded lens of hurts, failures, regrets, and rejections, we often struggle to see ourselves through our Creator's eyes. Those overwhelming feelings of inadequacy in our relationships and interactions become so frequent they feel natural. The lack of love for self turns into a lack of tolerance, grace, and forgiveness towards others. Worthy to receive love because we belong to Him, not because we have proven worthy to Him.

I encourage you to seek His Face and make your heart's desire to see yourself through his eyes. Where you are no longer bound by the fears of failure or the rejection and hurt from others. See yourself through the truth of being born again and adopted by the redeemer, loving yourself to love those around you genuinely. Empowered and emboldened walking in the knowledge that you were fearfully and wonderfully made! You have been called; you have been covered, redeemed, and now walk as one who has been restored!

Tarissa Williams

I declare
that my
health is
restored

You restored me to health and let me live. Surely it was for my benefit that I suffered such anguish. In your love you kept me from the pit of destruction; you have put all my sins behind your back.

Isaiah 38:16-17

JUNE 9

DECLARATION: I decree and declare that my mental, spiritual, and physical health is increased and I am welcomed, accepted and anointed to help women rebuke the spirit of depression proactively.

AFFIRMATION: I am strong, swift, and powerful; I run my race with purpose and perseverance, crushing the head of depression and hopelessness.

Depression is REAL and Christian women are not exempt from its grip. I faced a season of depression that felt like a series of upward climbs on a mountain with the roughest terrain you can imagine. Depression degraded me and draped me with a backpack of insecurities. Depression made me feel abandoned. In my mind, my presence was a burden. Depression worked overtime to isolate me. I spent most days in bed with soaked pillows and snotty tissues. I recreated darkness to accelerate the night by shutting the blinds in my room and my heart. You see, depression told me that I was not enough to face the light, use my gifts, or take steps into a season of wellness. I was hurting, and my spirit was parched, thirsty, and longing for an outpouring of soul-quenching showers.

Who would allow me to share my truth? Who would let me be vulnerable? Everyone I knew was proclaiming to be highly favored and exempt from troubles. In July 2010, while driving home from work, the idea of driving my Pathfinder off the bridge appealed to me. I was going to end it all because the idea of not having life figured out and the thought of doing life one more day was too much to bear. At that moment, I felt helpless and ashamed that this invisible burden blinded me to my future. My hands were shaking, but the moment my tires hit the yellow rumble strips, it all changed. I heard the voice of God say, "lift your head," I cried, and I screamed, I felt the presence of God hugging my soul and conditioning my weak heart; I felt love more powerful than any human being could provide. His presence has the power to reverse a curse and cancel the grip of depression. This was the day the stronghold of depression was broken from my life. I pulled my truck over, I worshipped, and at that moment, I understood that I was chosen and anointed for this, my mountain was my ministry.

Like the female deer whose hinds' feet, climbs rough and unpredictable terrain, I leap sure-footed up mountains (my past, heartbreak, rejection, fear, depression) without fear of losing my footing. Through prayer, reading, and listening to God's word concerning my life, I agree with God every morning. You may be looking at your mountain, unable to lift one foot in front of the other, you feel the heaviness of not having it all figured out. I want you to visualize the strong and sturdy hinds' feet, agile, strategic, and graciously fierce. By faith, we have the strength to climb the rough terrain of life. Together, we can take it one DAE at a time. You may feel exhausted and drained; He will give you rest. CLIMB. You may have to cry and walk and walk and cry; there is an intercessor in you. CLIMB. You may feel like you are losing your footing; He will reach for you and uphold you with His hand. CLIMB.

LaTisha Tippins

JUNE 10

Encouragement

Take the time to encourage yourself today. Write down
your wins for the month!

_____
_____
_____
_____
_____
_____
_____
_____
_____
_____
_____
_____
_____
_____

JUNE 11

DECLARATION: I decree and declare that God's plans for me are excellent.

AFFIRMATION: I am successful in everything God positions me to do.

Have you ever made plans for your life, and it didn't work out? Due to no manifestation, did you start to question God and yourself? I know this situation very well. Allow me to share how God revealed His promise in Jeremiah 29:11 to me. When it was time for me to go to college 28 years ago, I decided to major in Agricultural Economics because I wanted to finish what my late brother started. He was called home to be with the Lord during his Senior year in college. I thought that it was the ultimate tribute to him even though my interests were in the arts. I received my degree and went on to graduate school because I had a plan to establish a career in this field.

After leaving graduate school, I moved to the city and became a part of corporate America. After three years, I decided to move on to the hotel industry. I worked in the marketing & sales department. Within months, the entire department dismantled because my boss was embezzling money. I decided to work in the airline industry. Five months later, I was furloughed due to the slow season. It was at this point that I started to question my purpose. I knew that I was created to do more and serve others. I honestly didn't know what to do, except trust God. One night I prayed to God and told Him to let His will be done in my life. Two days later, I received a call for an interview with an organization in the agricultural arena. During the interview, the director and I recognized each other's names. I had spoken with him during my time as a marketing rep at the hotel. I realized that God had been working behind the scenes all along.

I felt empowered because I was finally working in my field. But unbeknownst to me, God had other plans for my life. My position allowed me to work with students in a school setting. I loved it! I loved it so much that I decided to become a teacher. My transition to education was so smooth that I knew it was God. I took the certification exams and passed them on the first try. I went to a job fair, and they hired me on the spot. I've been teaching currently for 14 years!

We can always plan things for ourselves, but God ultimately knows what's best for us. Sometimes our plans align with Him, and other times they don't. One thing's for sure. He will never leave us nor forsake us. When God is in it, failure is never an option.

Angela Kinnel

JUNE 12

DECLARATION: I decree and declare that God's purposes and plans for my life will prevail no matter the circumstance or issue that I may face.

AFFIRMATION: I am worthy, I am qualified, and I am the daughter of the one and only living God.

I am reminded of at time when I began to write each of my first two books. I thought of all the things that I hadn't gotten right in life. All the things that I really didn't want anyone to know out of fear. Fear of failure, fear of rejection, fear of shame, and embarrassment. I thought of being nineteen and pregnant out of wedlock from a drug dealer that I knew I wanted no future with. I thought of being pregnant a second time at twenty-one and having an abortion. I hid all the pain, guilt, and shame from my family. I thought about how I got pregnant some years later, not once but twice from a married man. I thought of the evictions and bankruptcies (three to be exact). I thought of all the harsh words and attitude, the way I would curse people out if they even looked at me wrong. Don't get me wrong there were many positive things that I had also accomplished, but when I was faced with coming forward and sharing who I am, I realized that the enemy has a way of highlighting only the negative.

If you find yourself feeling the way that I did, I've got good news. Therefore, there is no condemnation for those who are in Christ Jesus. (Romans 8:1 NIV) If any man is in Christ, he is a new creature; the old things have passed away behold all things have become new. I had to learn to forgive myself so that I could truly live. On the outside, I appeared strong and as if I had it all together. However, I was dying on the inside. God was ushering me into a new season, surrounded by ministerial and prophetic individuals. I was able to forgive others, but I was harboring resentment of who I knew myself to be. I was afraid of exposure of my past. As I prayed, God began to minister to me. We must show ourselves and others the grace of God because he wants us to be free so that we can live the life He destined for us.

Ephesians 1:7 tells us that in Him, we have redemption through his blood, the forgiveness of sin, in accordance with the riches of God's grace. The Holy Spirit said to me, "Not that we are competent in ourselves to claim anything for ourselves, but our competence comes from God". He has made us competent as ministers of a new covenant. We must hold our heads up and walk boldly into who God ordained us to be! God qualified me to share this testimony for the uplifting of his Kingdom, and He'll do the same for you!

Kathy Smith

JUNE 13

Prayer List

Take the time to pray for others today and put
their names below

_____

_____

_____

_____

_____

_____

_____

_____

_____

_____

_____

_____

_____

_____

I am
indestructible

JUNE 15

DECLARATION: I decree and declare that God's grace is sufficient to walk me through my pain and brokenness.

AFFIRMATION: I am not required to have it all together all the time; how glorious is that!

It took almost no time at all for the stick to report that I was pregnant. A dream that my husband and I have wanted for so long had finally come to pass. I went through many different ways that I wanted to reveal the happy news to my love. In the end, the setup didn't matter. All that mattered is that our family was growing. When he learned that we were expecting, he whispered, "I bet we're having twins." Which is what the OBGYN confirmed. The ultimate excitement that filled our hearts drowned the doctor's warning that one of the baby's heart rates was abnormal. "Let's wait and see," the doctor warned. With gumption and faith, my husband replied, "We serve a mighty God. He will take care of our baby. The baby will be healthy". We left the doctor's office with excitement for the journey we'd just embarked on—the journey to parenthood.

It was my mother that was with me at the next ultrasound appointment. My mother held my hand as we waited to see the pictures and hear the heartbeats. My mother squeezed my hand as the tears rolled when we learned that I had lost one child. When I met with my doctor, I asked the ridiculous questions -- did I not drink enough water; was it something that I did; did I somehow cause this miscarriage? Now it was time to consider how I would deliver the sad news to my love. Again, in the end, it didn't matter. Our focus now was on the baby that we still had.

Years before, my undergraduate college roommate told me I smiled before I woke up. She likened me to a Disney princess. I could always find the rainbow in the clouds. That is where I focused -- in happiness. I did the same here. How could I be sad when I had life growing inside of me? So what if we weren't having twins? So what if we did not get to have that dream? I focused on the joy, turning a blind eye to the grief of losing a baby. I refused to admit that I was angry at God for teasing us with this possibility. Ashamed that I indeed was hurt, that dark clouds would be a part of this story. "Rein in pain", I whispered in my heart. "Do not let your emotions hurt the baby that lives."

Sister, I can tell you with the strongest of convictions that God's grace is sufficient to walk us through any pain, brokenness, dark emotions we experience. He saw my suffering even as I denied its very existence and sent my circle of sisters to walk me through acknowledging the dark clouds, dealing with them, and heeding the lessons they had. As I surrendered being perfect to my mighty King, He comforted me. We do not have to smile all the time. They are seasons for tears. And sometimes, the tears and the smiles coexist.

Andrea Phillips

JUNE 16

DECLARATION: I decree and declare that I will look forward to a future of greatness with my eyes wide-open because I live a blessed life!

AFFIRMATION: I am no longer running from my history and the secrets and past hurts that had me enslaved to the feelings of unworthiness and self-loathing. "I am an overcomer!"

IIt was Monday, July 31, 2006, and I was so excited about the new life in front of me. The movers came the night before and packed up everything. I was so excited that I could hardly keep my eyes closed. I packed up my red 2004 Alero Oldsmobile, gave the leasing office my potted plant, said a prayer for safe travels, and took off without regret. After 31 years of living in Toledo, Ohio, I decided to brighten my horizons and see what would be waiting for me in Houston, Texas.

I was not just relocating; I was running away from painful memories that held me bound. I had memories of sexual fondling from family members, a rape from a previous boyfriend, an employer that sabotaged my reputation and fired me while I was in the recovery room after surgery, and debt up to my ears. I knew that life had more to offer me, and I finally muddled up the courage to start over again. True, my family did not quite understand the need for me to go so far away, but I knew that there was too much pain in that city.

After a decade of living in my new city, I still wound up in situations where I still had not confronted my past. One night, amid a drag-out fight with my then common-law husband, I decided to take my life. I took 22 pills and chased them with a bottle of Sangria while trying to slice my wrists. While I was in that hospital, I saw the Lord. He told me that I was better than this and that He truly loved me. It was then that I realized that I had a reason to live and experience the best that life had to offer without the pain of my past, without the opinion of others, and without fear.

It took less than a year to leave my abusive relationship, but it took years to detox from my past battle scars. Nothing that has happened to us is an accident or has taken God by surprise, and whatever we face is pruning us to help us develop the skills of resilience and bounce back that we are created to be in God's original design. He will send us the help that we need in the time of trouble. We must learn to study our triggers, resist the urge to run from our past, and confront the hard truths in a safe space so we can address them and move on with the help of those we trust to help us overcome.

Shaynne Witherspoon

JUNE 17

Beloved, I pray that all may go well with you and that you may be in good health, as it goes well with your soul.

3 John 1:2

JUNE 18

I create a calm household

JUNE 19

Prayer List

Take the time to pray for others today and put
their names below

_____

_____

_____

_____

_____

_____

_____

_____

_____

_____

_____

_____

_____

_____

_____

_____

JUNE 20

I am precious
to God

LORD, be gracious to us; we long for you. Be our strength every morning, our salvation in time of distress.

Isaiah 33:2

JUNE 22

Declarations

Take the time to declare victory in your life today. Write down your declarations for the month! We walk by faith and not by sight.

_____

_____

_____

_____

_____

_____

_____

_____

_____

_____

_____

_____

_____

_____

JUNE 23

DECLARATION: I decree and declare that no weapon formed against me shall prosper.

AFFIRMATION: I am a child of God and a follower of Jesus Christ, supplied with and protected by supernatural favor.

If you've ever experienced job loss before, you know how daunting and numbing it feels. The stress and the anxiety of not knowing or controlling what happens next. Not only in your career and finding new employment, but in your personal life and your finances. The feeling of failure even if you didn't do anything to contribute to your job loss. A few years ago when I lost my job it was painful, and I felt betrayed because I worked hard and invested a lot of my time in the role that I was in and, to be honest, my household could not sustain the loss of my job financially (or so I thought). After spending an exhausting number of hours, weeks, and days submitting job applications, interviewing, and networking, I started to journal not only my job search experience but also the experiences that I had been exposed to in my previous jobs both good and bad. The journal was intended for me to use as a tool to reflect on and better myself as a professional through the lessons that I had learned through my experiences.

The more I journaled, the more I realized that God had been teaching me through the experiences that I had to help me grow spiritually and to grow closer to Him. It took me losing a job and journaling to realize that God was right there with me in the workplace, an environment where we're conditioned to believe God doesn't have a place. As I prayed and journaled, God placed it on my heart to share my experiences with other professionals and invite Him into their workspace and careers. It was through this revelation that my first book was birthed. During this time, God sustained my household; we didn't miss a bill payment or a meal. God also blessed me with a new job that allowed me to grow professionally, and that spoke more to His purpose for me than the job I had previously lost. The enemy attacks us in many different ways to make us want to shrink back, dim our lights, and lose sight of our identity in Christ to pull us away from our Father. We've all doubted God and have allowed the enemy to drown out His strong, yet still and quiet voice speaking into our lives. The good news is that God never stops speaking to us; we have to be more intentional about taking the time to hear Him.

Once I reached out to God, asked Him to dress me in His spiritual armor, drew closer to Him, and asked for prayer from my tribe of prayer warriors; God showed me that He was always right there fighting for me, even when my faith wavered. The war rages on for each of us, but your faith in God is all you need to win the battle. No matter how hard the fight, no matter how many times you get knocked down and how hard it may be to get back up, know that your Father, who breathed life into you at your conception and gave you a new life through His only begotten son has your back, and He won't allow any weapon formed against you to prosper!

Sonya Sneed-Scott

I am God's workmanship

I possess the qualities needed to be extremely successful

Peace I leave with you; my peace I give you. I do not give to you as the world gives. Do not let your hearts be troubled and do not be afraid.

John 14:27

JUNE 27

I forgive those who have harmed me in the past

JUNE 28

Encouragement

Take the time to encourage yourself today. Write down your wins for the month!

_____

_____

_____

_____

_____

_____

_____

_____

_____

_____

_____

_____

_____

_____

JUNE 29

I base my happiness on blessings that I've been given

<u>JUNE 30</u>

My flesh and my heart may fail, but God is the strength of my heart and my portion forever.

Psalm 73:26

July

JULY 1

Goal Setting

Use today to set your goals for the year.
Be clear and specific with what you want to achieve.
Break the goal down into steps.
All the best in achieving your goals this year!

_____

_____

_____

_____

_____

_____

_____

_____

_____

_____

_____

_____

JULY 2

DECLARATION: I decree and declare that the love of God in my heart brings all the right people into my life for every real purpose.

AFFIRMATION: I am prosperous in everything I do and I am the master of all of the good things that God puts into my life, but nothing is the master of me.

One of my defining moments in my life is when I was verbally and physically abused. At that moment, I was shocked and enraged all at the same time. For me, the pain was nothing I've ever experienced before. I was overwhelmed with what I was feeling, that numbing feeling from the inside. I felt humiliated and ashamed that I didn't speak up or fight back. It took a toll on my mental health that I thought this was healthy. Healthy because people get into arguments, get upset, and say things that they don't mean but do our best to work through the mistake of our actions.

No, this was different, different in the way of being attacked by my character, my disposition of where I was at in life, name-calling you name it, it was hell for me. I ask myself, How did I get to this low point in my life that I would allow this to happen? Did so-called love genuinely blind me? No, that can't be it. I knew better. I could no longer sit in pain and in the silence of confused feelings of Why's and How come. I was truly mentally exhausted by hurt and disappointment and feeling guilty all the time. I was tired of feeling imprisoned by my emotions of despair by not feeling as if I was good enough, not worthy enough by the lack of someone else's shortcomings and past traumas. I knew I had to pull myself out of the deep murky waters to heal again. To forgive myself was the most important of all, to be that loving and happy person that I've always been and will continue to be.

I had to do it not only for myself but for my child's sake. I never wanted my child to see or feel the sadness that I was going through. I needed help and, I'm so grateful for it because it would not have made me the strong woman I am today. Today I am much more reliable than I was before. Wiser to be careful of the signs. That season of life took one day at a time. One day to accept and forgive me for not knowing my worth. Days to process and see that it's not my fault and time to heal all my broken places and become whole again.

We all have challenges in life that we must overcome. Lord knows it is not natural but essential to move forward in life, and you'll be so much happier for it. Your peace is so vital to you and never let anyone take that away. My hope and prayer are that I have reached you not to feel like you're walking alone in silence and pain, but to speak up and seek help. It's not too late for you to have all the happiness and love in the world that you so desire. You deserve it. I pray that this blesses and encourages you to heal every broken and crooked place you thought was imaginable to reach and fulfilled by the love of God. You're not alone.

Devin Ross

I am courageous and I stand up for myself

Today, I abandon my old habits and take up new, more positive ones

Jesus went through all the towns and villages, teaching in their synagogues, proclaiming the good news of the kingdom and healing every disease and sickness

Matthew 9:35

JULY 6

DECLARATION: I decree and declare that God is at my right hand, and I will not be shaken.

AFFIRMATION: I am delivered from the spirit of fear.

The testimony that I'm about to share demonstrates how refusing to walk in fear allows the finished work of Jesus to manifest in your life. Almost ten years ago, I received an upper respiratory infection diagnosis. My physician prescribed antibiotics and rest. After two weeks, I was not feeling any better. I went back to visit my physician. He ordered a chest x-ray. Within minutes after the x-ray, I received a referral to see a pulmonary specialist with no other explanation. During my first visit with the specialist, he informed me that there was a spot on my right lung.

While explaining the location on the x-ray slides, I was having a whole conversation in my mind saying, "a spot? What? In my lung? Cancer? Benign or Malignant? Father God, no!" Other tests had to be completed. I left that office feeling nervous and overwhelmed. But I quickly directed my attention to the Lord in prayer. I understood that for me to deal with this, I could not walk in fear. I had to stay calm and confident that the stripes of Jesus already healed me. I affirmed that I was not walking in the spirit of anxiety each day, and I was healed. Negative thoughts from the enemy tried to enter, but I rebuked them. About two weeks later, I had another appointment with the specialist. He decided to do another chest x-ray. Twenty minutes later, he walked in, made a sigh as he sat down, and said, "Ms. Kinnel, the spot is gone!"

I laughed because I knew what had manifested. All I could do was thank the Lord. The doctor was in disbelief. I am a witness to the fact that we don't have to walk in fear of anything. The phrase "fear not" is used 80 times in the Bible. God knew that He had to repeatedly remind us not to fear because the enemy attempts to use fear to reduce our faith in the Lord. God is our source, our refuge, and our peace.

All we have to do is believe, trust, and speak His promises over our lives. His word is life to our mind, body, and spirit. We have what we say! Proclaim this with me today, "NO FEAR HERE, IN THE NAME OF JESUS!"

Angela Kinnel

JULY 7

Encouragement

Take the time to encourage yourself today. Write down your wins
for the month!

_____

_____

_____

_____

_____

_____

_____

_____

_____

_____

_____

_____

_____

_____

_____

_____

_____

JULY 8

DECLARATION: I decree and declare that I am in full agreement with God's plan for my life and I am at peace with His plan. My heart is not troubled, and I am not afraid.

AFFIRMATION: I am walking in freedom, and I am no longer weighed down by others' opinions.

This is my current situation! I started agreeing with God, and my life has never been the same. Fully coming in agreement with my Heavenly Father has propelled me into my newfound truth and has caused me to move beyond others' opinions. I am no longer walking around carrying unnecessary baggage. I am much lighter and no longer concerned about marching to the beat of others. I have been set free, and so can you! We can take this journey together. Unfortunately, I could not share this life-changing news a few years ago. I could not testify to something that ticked me off every time I talked about it. I spent a little over 15 years pleasing others and not tapping into my true calling. I did not have a clear understanding of my purpose. Honestly, I could not walk in my calling for being what others expected me to be. Taking on the expectations of others led me to many detours and roadblocks. My life did not feel like it belonged to me or even to God.

I knew that something had to change. When I expressed my concerns to my grandmother, I did not get the response I was desperately searching for. She stated that it was up to me to change it. She then asked a soul seeking question that caused me to dig a little deeper. She asked me, "How long are you going to allow others to mistreat you and manipulate you?" My turning point was shortly after our phone conservation. In 2018, I finally got the courage to change what I was not pleased with. I viewed my journal and circled every time that I wanted to say "no," but said, "yes." I counted the cost and found that my "now" behavior was too costly and prevented me from hearing, being, and doing.

Today is the day that we actively take one step at a time. It is time to stop marching to the beat of others and find your rhythm that God designed. You can get engaged in seeing the results by making some small changes. Change is never easy. Someone will always be offended over your choices. It is not going to be easy, but it is necessary to move beyond. You have been in this position for far too long. Praise the Lord! You are coming out! Ask God for help and surround yourself with people who appreciate you. Moving forward with the help of the Lord and view past mistakes as learning opportunities. We can embrace our journey without fear of how others will see our decisions. You do not have to worry about not fitting in or belonging. You are a part of God's family, and you are loved.

Declaring God's Word is essential to do daily. Studying Ephesians helped me and will help you identify who you are and what your purpose is. Come into full agreement with God and watch things turn around and work out in your favor.

Cheryl Bryant

I am a powerhouse; I am indestructible

And the people all tried to touch him, because power was coming from him and healing them all.

Luke 6:19

I declare that though these times are difficult, they are only a short phase of life

JULY 12

Prayer List

Take the time to pray for others today and
put their names below

_____

_____

_____

_____

_____

_____

_____

_____

_____

_____

_____

_____

_____

_____

_____

_____

_____

_____

I radiate beauty, charm, and grace.

I declare that I am conquering my obstacles

JULY 15

Something new

Do something new today that you haven't done before. Talk about your experience below.

_____

_____

_____

_____

_____

_____

_____

_____

_____

_____

_____

_____

_____

_____

_____

JULY 16

DECLARATION: I decree and declare that the limits that cause me to compare myself to others are removed today.

AFFIRMATION: I am uniquely created to be the best me.

Growing up, I was always a different one. I was stripes and polka dots together kind of girl well before it was the "In" trend. I was always a different chick in the group. Yes, I was the fruit loop in the world of cheerios! Especially as an adolescent, people would not include me in the group because they know I would do things a bit differently. I often wondered why I must think so differently, why I must see the world so differently. In my early 20's, I lost who I was for a few years simply because I was different and didn't fit in. I wanted to be "normal" according to others' rules, but as much as I tried, I failed every time.

I was consumed with a fear of failure, fear of what other people think, and a fear of rejection. I began to live in a box of insecurities, which caused me to try to live up to standards that were created by man. You know those standards; bone straight hair is in, a size 4 is a perfect size, light-skinned is in, the love of rainbows means you are gay. Satan was in my head and began to cause confusion and water those seeds of failure and rejection. He caused me to lose focus and vision of who I was, whom God created me to be. Just in perfect time, I remember a truth statement that my middle school teacher spoke into my life many years prior. Her truth statement was, "You were not created to be a duplicate but an original." It was indeed a true statement that counteracted everything Satan had caused me to believe.

From that moment on, I decided that I was going to be ME! The me that God created! Yes, the quirky, brown-skinned, size 22 with kinky hair girl that loves rainbows and glitter. I was going to be the unique, bold, fun-loving chick that he created me to be. It was time to bury the standards of being a duplication. I started living as an original and being the beYOUtiful me. Have you been living by the standards that you are not normal? Have you thought I am not pretty like her? Have you ever said if I had her body, I would...(fill in the blank)?

Today is our day to stop living as a duplicate and live as a priceless original. We have been beautifully designed; we are the master's piece! We are a limited edition, beYOUtiful always. We have been fearfully and wonderfully made in his image. Today is the day we stand up and say, no, I am not normal. I have been created to be uniquely me. Today is the day we stand up and say no, I do not look like her, but good God I am pretty in the skin I am in. Today we stand and say I am beYOUtiful because I am uniquely me!

Shenay Lewis-Hairston

JULY 17

Prayer List

Take the time to pray for others today and put their names below

_____

_____

_____

_____

_____

_____

_____

_____

_____

_____

_____

_____

_____

_____

_____

JULY 18

DECLARATION: I decree and declare that the strength of my ancestors will continue through my bloodline, and through Christ Jesus, I will encourage and support every woman to stand in her wholeness despite the loss of a child.

AFFIRMATION: I am chosen to stand firm after the loss of a child.

December 1994, a high-risk pregnancy, stationed in North Dakota, doctors determined that I needed a medical evacuation to Virginia to determine if my pregnancy would be sustainable. I was required to leave my then seven-year-old behind to be cared for by friends for almost three months. I finally returned home, and two weeks later, I awoke, and I immediately knew something was wrong. Keeping my focus was vital. I didn't want my daughter to know that anything was wrong. I got her off to school and headed to the hospital. It wasn't long before they confirmed my worst fears. I had miscarried in my seventh month. How do I go home and tell my daughter she would never meet her baby sister? I carried my baby five more days to allow my body to prepare for delivery naturally. Inside I was breaking down, trying not to wail out loud. I spent those days on my knees, praying for God to carry me through this. I was in total despair, and I felt I could not get through this. I begged him to give me strength.

I had to survive because I had another child that needed me. I delivered in a hospital room alone, they came in and handed her to me. Her head went back, and she seemed to gasp for air, I looked at the nurse, and she assured me, it was just a reflex. I was sure if I just breathed air into her lungs, she would take a breath, and it would all be a dream. I knew it was real. She was gone. My heart was breaking into a million pieces. "Why was this not meant to be"? I held her checking her fingers, her toes, her eyes – she was beautiful. My heart hurt to know it was the last time that I would hold her and gaze upon her face. But slowly, at that moment, I felt peace. I had prayed, and I knew God had taken his angel home with him because he had another plan for me. Today, because of that experience, I feel empathy, I feel stronger, I know my worth, I am a conqueror. One day at a time, we will get back to normal; through counseling, therapy, connecting with others who share our story. Write letters to your lost love, journal your thoughts, pray, and permit yourself to cry and feel. Take time, talk with family, friends, find peace. You will find passion again for living, to volunteer, to give back and support others.

To every woman, through joy, pain, and devastation, we build character. Know that God has a plan for your life, and he is holding you every step of the way. You will make it! You are amazing, beautiful, reliable, and your light will continue to shine. You are blessed! For every woman who has struggled in motherhood, accept the challenges, disappointments, and moments of inadequacy, knowing that you are powerful.

Toni Chavis

I declare that my life is just beginning.

I declare that my fears of tomorrow are simply melting away.

JULY 21

DECLARATION: I decree and declare that I am whole in my soul.

AFFIRMATION: I am worthy of all that God has prepared for me.

After accepting the fact that my marriage was over, it was time to focus on healing. This was indeed a one "DAE" at a time moment. A major challenge was silencing the thought that I wasn't worth fighting for. It wasn't that I felt unworthy, or had low self-esteem, for I know who I am in Christ, and that my identity comes from Him alone. Nor was it from my ex, for we were cordial towards one another. We just couldn't agree on how to fix our issues, and without agreement, there's no power, and no covenant.

We know Satan uses division, so without a strong foundation of uniting in prayer, which I believe fortifies oneness in the spirit, or singleness of heart, we handed our marriage to him on a silver platter. This is the result of broken trust, which a remedy for that is uniting in prayer for it helps you see one another through the eyes of God. Holy Spirit can then teach you how to relate to one another, and you can combat any outside influences, fears, insecurities and yes, selfishness.

I was disappointed and felt betrayed, but realized that sometimes those we love don't recognize who we are, nor the value we add to their lives, so let them go! God has given us the right to choose, and He doesn't override that. I resolved to add this experience to my list of lessons learned and moved on. Know that you can too. If you so desire, and you trust God, He'll present you before another. He'll be there for you, and is the only one you can rely on no matter what. I remember reading His promise of never (under any circumstance) will He desert you, give up on you, or leave you without support. Nor will He relax His hold on you, rest assured.

He's made us royalty, so our worth has already been determined. All we have to do now is carry ourselves as such. Accepting nothing less than honor and respect from those we allow to enter into our lives. See yourself as a victor, not a victim, so you can embrace your new beginning being much wiser and stronger. Let's not bring baggage into our new relationships. Let's take the time and put in the work to become whole ourselves, so we'll attract another whole person.

You deserve a loving, devoted King who isn't threatened by a Queen. One who understands that you'll rule together, being a safe place for one another as your lives shine to make an impact in this world.

Fonda Kelly

I am at peace with all that has happened, is happening, and will happen.

JULY 23

DECLARATION: I decree and declare that I am beautifully and wonderfully made in the eye of our creator.

AFFIRMATION: I am BIG (Bold. Intentional. Godly).

My life in itself is a story full of pain, abandonment, strength, and triumph! Through my life's experiences, I was able to find my life's passion and discover the true Queen that lies within, and I believe that's in all of us. I had to reinvent myself, and that's when Ebonique Hebb had arrived. This story is a testimony to the value of life's turbulent times and the power to step out on faith and trust God and His process. The best part is how I desire to teach and give back the lessons I've learned.

Born in Detroit, Michigan, to a single mother, I was a fatherless child. I grew up as a child with many questions, like where was this other piece to my puzzle? My mother and I moved to Baltimore, Maryland, when I was four. It was the beginning of twists and turns in my life, including the start of molestation at the age of four and constant rejection by family members, especially the women in my life. Feelings of insecurity, fear, and low self- esteem set in. I had no idea how it would shape my future and also affect my children. I started to peel back layers of generational curses one by one, one DAE at a time with God's grace. By age 17, I was a teenage mother. I thought, what would I do with a child at 17? Growing up from a childhood of pain, rejection, and generational curses can cause one to make many bad decisions, which was the case for me. Four years later, after many of those bad decisions, I became a mother again at 22. I started to make an accurate evaluation of my life. I didn't want my children to suffer from the same fate that happened to me. I became devoted to raising my two girls to be great women.

I use prayer and meditation as my constant refuge. I became a true believer in self-soothing and God's mighty power. WE ARE VICTORIOUS, AND IT'S NOT WHERE WE CAME FROM, IT'S ABOUT WHERE WE ARE GOING. A wise man told me a long time ago. "Gold doesn't shine until it's gone through the fire." I turned my pain into my purpose. I started seeking healthy relationships with women, I removed anything unhealthy, and I prayed for keen discernment. You have to sit back and breathe, trust God's process, and know that He has a purpose for your life.

Remember, you are beautifully and wonderfully made in the eye of the beholder. Say to yourself that you are enough. You are courageous and loved by God. Give yourself a break and forgive yourself for not knowing how amazing you indeed are. Freedom is knocking on the door, and it's there if you want it.

Ebony Hebb

JULY 24

Encouragement

Take the time to encourage yourself today. Write down your
wins for the month!

_____

_____

_____

_____

_____

_____

_____

_____

_____

_____

_____

_____

_____

_____

_____

_____

JULY 25

I acknowledge my own self-worth: my confidence is soaring.

Today, I abandon my old habits and take up new, more positive ones.

JULY 27

Journal

This simple practice improves mental clarity, offers the ability to see the big picture of our lives, and serves as a catalogue of every success we've ever had.

_____

_____

_____

_____

_____

_____

_____

_____

_____

_____

_____

_____

_____

_____

_____

_____

I am

courageous

My business
is growing,
expanding,
and thriving.

Heal me, O LORD, and I shall be healed; save me, and I shall be saved, for you are my praise

Jeremiah 17:14

JULY 31

Encouragement

Take the time to encourage yourself today.
Write down your wins for the month!

_____

_____

_____

_____

_____

_____

_____

_____

_____

_____

_____

_____

_____

_____

_____

August

AUGUST 1

DECLARATION: I decree and declare that the strongholds of perversion, oppression, and injustice are destroyed, and my burdens are lifted.

AFFIRMATION: I am clothed with strength and dignity; I laugh without fear of the future.

I was born in the Mississippi Delta in the early '60s, during a time of turmoil and unrest across our Nation. The Civil Rights movement was taking shape all around me. I was raised in a Christian home, and as much as my parents loved me, as a young child, I was left to raise myself. Sadly, I became easy prey for sexual predators. At around the age of five, I was molested by a family member. Later, I was molested by what we now call a neighborhood sex offender. Seeds of deception, manipulation, perversion, discrimination, low self-esteem and low self-worth were planted in me. My innocence and youth said good girls didn't do such things; they didn't speak up or bring attention. Just pretend it never happened. I learned to place them in my little mental box, put a lid on it, and carefully tuck it away. Unfortunately, the things I'd placed in the box did not lie dormant. As I grew older, the seeds of perversion that had been planted in me grew, took on other forms and manifested in different ways. The need to feel accepted, validated, and loved was overwhelming, and I became promiscuous in college. While my pride said I would never be labeled a victim of anything, as an adult in my early 40s, I was sexually harassed by my supervisor and raped by a family friend.

I felt worthless, ashamed, embarrassed, alone, and trapped. I was miserable inside, even when it seemed, I had everything, and everything was in order. I had a loving husband, two beautiful children, a promising career, my dream home, owned a business, and had a bright future. But my identity and security were situated atop my box filled with secrets and lies. I hadn't recognized it then, but now I understand that this was the source of restlessness, depression, and suicidal thoughts that I could never pinpoint or fully understand. That eventually led to problems in my marriage. On top of everything else, I'd been deceived. The enemy had turned my life upside down. I'd hit rock bottom and couldn't find any answers. I cried out to God, and He gave me a revelation! The inner peace and spiritual wholeness I'd sought all my life would never come until I acknowledged it, sought help, and exposed the secrets and lies the enemy thrived on. In that moment of surrender, I felt the weight and burdens of my past. Those burdens that I had carried all my life, finally lifted off of my shoulders. I felt a freedom and spiritual awakening that I had never experienced. I felt an assurance that healing and deliverance was my portion.

God will give you PEACE, HOPE, and the STRENGTH to do what you thought you could never do. He will strengthen you to expose the enemy and walk out your deliverance. God is so faithful! No matter what is tormenting us from our past and no matter how long it has been hidden, we can be delivered.

Monica Williams

AUGUST 2

Use today to set your goals for the year.
Be clear and specific with what you want to achieve.
Break the goal down into steps.
All the best in achieving your goals this year!

_____

_____

_____

_____

_____

_____

_____

_____

_____

_____

_____

_____

_____

I forgive those who have harmed me in my past and peacefully detach from them

AUGUST 4

DECLARATION: I decree and declare that I forgive myself for past, present, and future pains.

AFFIRMATION: I am able to administer the love of Christ to myself, my family, and those who come in my path.

I'm here to encourage you through the guilt, shame, and unforgiveness that I carried for so long. Losing my mom July 4th, 2019, was a transition in my life. Being realistic, I was broken, bitter, hurt, and angry inside, and nobody could tell me how to feel. Losing my queen was a tough pill to swallow and to accept for a while. I was heavily burdened, not knowing how to deal with some much inside. It felt like a replay of when I lost my father at the age of 15. Until my early 20s, my mom and I, our bond, started to become better. I had so much anger towards her because I felt like if she was there raising me and not trying to provide, I wouldn't have had to raise myself. I sometimes looked at her as being a person I blamed instead of forgiving her and loving her the way I should.

 The day I got the call from my sister Terrica that she was dead was devastating. She passed in her sleep at home with my sister. I felt so bad because I blamed myself for some of the pain that he carried, that's where the guilt came in. How could her daughter, who she loved and supported, be so upset with her? I didn't know how to forgive her, and after her passing, I prayed and let her know, "Mommy, I forgive you," and I forgive myself for hurting you, I had guilt on my shoulder. I didn't know how to accept God's will at first, even with my family support, friends, and church family.

At times it just didn't feel like it was enough. I had my times of going back and easing the pain with marijuana; I used it to cope with what I was going through. I felt I didn't want to talk to anyone. I was praying and crying out to God because I was so broken. I would meditate on that scripture in Psalms 51:17 the holy spirit leads me there one day, and it says, "The sacrifices of God are a broken spirit; a broken and contrite heart, O God, you WILL NOT despise". He allowed me to see his perspective that he allowed me to snap to mold me into being more like him; I had begun the process of surrendering completely. I started my healing and acceptance stage in Feb 2020, and I began praying to GOD to help me get my strength back and help me accept His will so that I could adequately heal and overcome this. I was ready to move on with my life.

I want to encourage anyone that If you are dealing with unforgiveness, guilt, and shame about anything, give your burdens to GOD. I'm grateful I was able at a young age of 29 to get it right with him now. No matter what age you are, you can still get it right. Don't beat yourself up or put yourself down. David was young, and he always did great things for the Kingdom of God.

Katera Shannon

My body is healthy; my mind is brilliant; my soul is tranquil.

I am the architect of my life

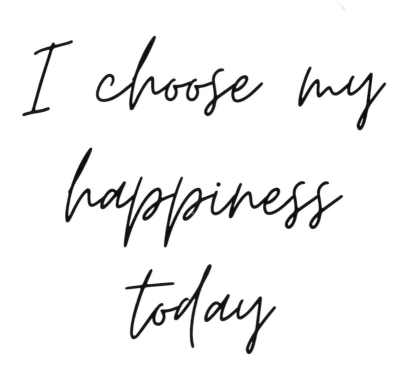

I choose my happiness today

AUGUST 8

DECLARATION: I decree and declare that God can use me in any situation I find myself in and move me toward my purpose.

AFFIRMATION: I am more than a diagnosis.

I woke up and felt my unborn baby kicking in my stomach. I was cold, lonely, and depressed. My first night in the psychiatric hospital, all I could think about was how I was a terrible mother, an awful mother, and a terrible mother spending my last trimester of pregnancy thinking about suicide. No one ever talks to you about the horrors that pregnant mothers face. Before I had my first child, I had never heard of postpartum depression, let alone antepartum depression. Here I was dealing with this mental health disorder, all alone. I was in the psychiatric hospital on involuntary commitment for five days because a psychiatrist and judge deemed that I was a risk to myself.

On the third day, I remember sitting at my desk in my room, and I had the idea to write to my children. I wrote letters telling them how proud of them I was, and that when I left this facility, I would do everything I could to surrender to God to rule & reign over my life. The last letter I wrote was to my unborn baby, where I asked him for forgiveness, compassion, and empathy if he ever found out that I was in this position during the last couple of months of my pregnancy with him. When I finished writing the letters, I asked God to give my baby an unspeakable joy, even though I had none throughout my pregnancy with him. I ran across a scripture earlier that day that summarized my desperate plea to God, Psalm 30:5.

Ironically, I cried like a newborn baby when I read that scripture. Seven years later, my son is one of the most joyous boys I have ever met. My son's joy counteracts with any struggle or setback we have faced in our family over the years. My family and I affectionately call him, "Jolly Jeremiah." My son is the personification of joy. God answered my prayers. God has shown me countless times during my battle with depression that he can exchange my sadness to joyfulness! God provides sustenance in my heart, and he filled the void in my spirit when I was so fearful of how my baby's life would enter in the world due to my depressive disposition. God turned my pain into power! I became empowered despite my circumstances, and in the end, allowed me to see a new life come into this world, my son.

I am a Licensed Clinical Social Worker, and I will soon be a Registered Nurse working in the psychiatric mental health field. In the fall, I will start in the Psychiatric Mental Health Nurse Practitioner Program at Vanderbilt University. The Lord took me from being a psychiatric patient to a psychiatric provider, and He can do the same for you. He will move you from the victim to the victor. We can trade our sorrow for joy!

April McLamb

AUGUST 9

DECLARATION: I decree and declare that I will always have enough of the right resources, the right attitude, and the right mindset.

AFFIRMATION: I am enough, regardless of what happens around me, to hold me down or keep me from accomplishing my purpose.

As each new day begins, I will reach inside to use my most powerful resource. That resource is from the source that lies within and empowers me daily. Whenever I feel challenged or inadequate throughout my day, I say this affirmation aloud and with resolve. For every defeating moment and thought, I remind myself, I AM Enough. I know that my words, when spoken, are deposited into me. And as soon as I declare that I am enough in any situation, things start to shift. I am now manifesting my dreams. I am retraining my thoughts and beliefs that allow me to attract the life I once wished for. All of this was started with affirming myself to myself daily. I am grateful that once I stopped comparing and started complimenting myself, things began to change. Reminding me that I am enough, also meant that I didn't need to compare myself with anyone else. I boldly proclaim that I am enough, even when self-doubt starts to creep in when I decide to take on a new task or begin to doubt whether I have what it takes to finish an old task.

I AM Enough reaffirms that my self-esteem is high and that I have what it takes to succeed. This affirmation also allows for meaningful existence within and to those connected to us. By declaring who we are, we subconsciously give others, such as our family, peers, and others in society, to experience the same. By using this affirmation, we drive out any negative thoughts that may creep in. Fundamentally, the more you use the affirmation, I AM ENOUGH, the more powerful those words become. Those words begin to become deeply rooted in who you are becoming. Positive self-talk helps old and unhelpful thoughts and behavior patterns. By affirming that you are enough, you increase the possibility of what you can do and what you can create.

By saying I am enough, you are also speaking to yourself that you have everything you need inside of you. It rewires your thoughts and heart for gratitude and love of self. It evokes positive feelings, positive intentions, which fuels positive actions. Those words, along with other affirmations, offer endless options on who or what you can become. By repeating these words aloud or silently, you can begin to embody all you are seeking. The days of not knowing which direction to begin will start with having a set mindset, that I am enough. The foundational thought of our daily existence will provide us with enough to keep us grounded in what we are saying and believing for ourselves. Release the negative thoughts, receive the greatness on the inside and begin to accept that YOU ARE ENOUGH.

Inetta Bunn

AUGUST 10

Encouragement

Take the time to encourage yourself today.
Write down your wins for the month!

_____
_____
_____
_____
_____
_____
_____
_____
_____
_____
_____
_____
_____
_____
_____
_____

I am grateful for the good things in my life

AUGUST 12

Prayer List

Take the time to pray for others today and put their names below

AUGUST 13

The righteous cry out,
and the LORD hears
them; he delivers them
from all their troubles.
The LORD is close to the
brokenhearted and
saves those who are
crushed in spirit.

Psalm 34:17-18

AUGUST 14

I deserve
prosperity
and freedom

I am creative
and open to
new ideas

AUGUST 16

DECLARATION: I decree and declare that I walk in the divine purpose and will of God for my life and that all generational curses of abuse are broken, and my seed shall see the salvation of the Lord.

AFFIRMATION: I am a valuable, worthy, and capable woman of God, equipped to be what God intended for me to become.

As I begin to examine and identify the core reason, I felt unworthy, rejected, and even abandoned. I realized that I was just a young girl looking for love everywhere and failed to find it. On this long journey, I'd searched and hoped that someone would love and accept me. In the summer of 1999, my bedroom was gloomy, cold, and all of the shades were down. Wrapped in an old faded pink and white terry cloth robe, I found myself. My children were in their rooms. I was so unhappy and miserable. As I laid curled up in bed, I was mean and bitter and did not want to be bothered.

However, as I struggled to find me, I ended up hiding me. Unfortunately, I was good at hiding. In hiding, I even hid the abuse I suffered along the way. I was naïve and clueless about who I was. I left home and became a wife at nineteen. Then loneliness and rejection turned into bitterness and anger. I was bitter and unhappy, still trying to find me! Not knowing myself caused me to harbor the thought of being a failure as a young mother.

Consequently, my children and I experienced abuse. This abuse was reverting. I felt horrible, embarrassed, shameful, guilty, insufficient, and prideful. Yes, pride would not let me express or reveal the magnitude of my pain. I recall crying for days, that turned into nights, that evolved into months, which soon became routine. I knew I had to find a way of escape for my children and me. The true me was invisible. The pain developed into unforgiveness and bitterness! Life seemed awkward, and more than anything, I felt insufficient, rejected, and abandoned. I felt shattered!

One day God came in, and I was able to muster up a small glimpse of hope and embrace who God had created me to be. I knew I had to find a way of escape for my children and me. I began to run hard after the Lord. Through this journey, I had unwrapped and exposed that part of me that was capable, loved, and valued. That was extremely hard to digest. I struggled with the thought that if the Lord loved me, why would He let me experience so much pain!

On April 12, 2019, the Lord woke me up, and I began to journal my pain. I began to face me. My anxiety began to surface. I journaled what the Lord placed in my heart, and my why changed to why not? We have to believe in God's word about us. That's when the light will start to shine, and you will be able to hold your head up high. You can face your pain and brokenness and change your thinking of why me to why not me?

Trinnette Greene

I am in control of my thoughts

My life is a process and I accept change

Gracious words are a
honeycomb, sweet to
the soul and healing to
the bones

Proverbs 16:24

AUGUST 20

DECLARATION: I decree and declare that I will war over the words that were previously spoken over me while holding fast to my faith.

AFFIRMATION: I am chosen to stake the territory God has God me to pursue.

There are very few things I share with others about my life. These are things I choose to forget. Yet, they have shaped the destiny that God has me pioneering. As a young girl, I was bullied in junior high. I remember kids who would put gum in my hair and would get on their knees and bark at me like a dog. The humiliation I felt was deep. I cried when I got home. I had so much anxiety. I hated going to school. Yet, I knew I needed to keep going no matter what. I never understood why.

I always had that timid spirit, but yet I had to deal with it. Was it because of my color? Was it because of my disability, or was it because the enemy knew the territory I would pursue? This went on for two years. It finally got to the point of my schedule completely changed. Classes were harder. That same year a talent show was taking place. I chose to sing a song with words that said, "If he carried the weight of the word upon his shoulder, I know my brother and sister, he will carry you." Those same kids that bullied me, gave standing ovation.

All my life I dealt with a learning disability. I fought a timid spirit. I was never the best test taker. Some things took me a little longer. I never felt like I had leadership qualities. Some days I really felt like I would never amount to anything. I constantly fought that timid spirit. The anxiety would build, but I chose to confront the fears. I was not going to let it rule my life. I pursued college and graduated. Finally, it took losing my keys too many times to get answers. At the age of 28, I was diagnosed with ADHD. The more I began to learn about myself, the more I realized I was smart. The light bulb came on. The faith that resonated within me all of sudden caused me to let the enemy know what authority I was given and responsibility I had to carry out.

That same faith, as mentioned in I Timothy 6:12, that says 'fight the good fight of faith" was a tool that God had given to war over the prophecies previously spoken over me (I Tim 1:18-19). That same faith is within you. You have been given the challenge to stake your territory. Use the authority to let the enemy know you were charged with the responsibility given by God to carry your assignment.

Dani Tredway

AUGUST 21

DECLARATION: I decree and declare that I will break the generational curse in my family.

AFFIRMATION: I am healthy and more than a multiple sclerosis diagnosis. I am the evidence of God's healing power.

In 2015, I lost one of my best friends, Charlett. She was more like my older sister. I watched as cancer slowly took her away. I had lost people who were close to me before. But there was something different about my sister's transition. It felt as if a part of me had been taken away. Before I realized it, I found myself grieving in a way I never experienced before. Nobody would have even known. I still functioned as my usual self. I went to work. I attended social events with friends. I was also starting to speak at women's empowerment seminars. However, deep inside, I was spiraling into a state of depression. When it all finally hit me, I was in the hospital being evaluated. I had a nervous breakdown. Even I couldn't believe it. Not me. Carla – the strong one. It was at my weakest moment that I realized I was not as strong as neither I nor others thought I was. The doctors ordered an MRI of my brain to determine what caused my behavior.

The results revealed three lesions on my brain. I immediately panicked, thinking it could be cancer. After all, that's what took my sister less than a year prior. The doctors told me it could be multiple sclerosis. Every emotion raced through me. I was terrified. I did not even want to get further tested to determine whether the diagnosis was for sure. You see, my cousin had been diagnosed with multiple sclerosis. I saw how debilitating the disease was in her body. She had to use a walker to assist with her mobility. Her condition was all I knew about the disease. I did not want to go through that. I could not go through that. I wanted to be physically capable of attending my son's college graduation. I needed to be healthy enough to see my daughter graduate from high school. I had too much to do. I held off for as long as I could. I prayed for God to give me the strength to endure whatever the outcome was going to be. I scheduled a spinal tap that revealed I did indeed have multiple sclerosis.

What seemed at first like a devastatingly horrible situation was one the best blessings of my life. Often, we can't see the good in our situation because it hurts. But God sometimes has to shake us and take us through trials and tribulations. He might even take something away from us so we can see Him. I believe God slowed me down through Charlett's death and my diagnosis so I can hear from Him. Maybe you didn't lose a close friend or get a life-changing diagnosis. Perhaps you volunteer for everything and are always busy. He wants to get your attention so you can live out your purpose, and He gets all the Glory. Let Him! I did, and I am so grateful I made that choice.

Carla Hills

The people in my life love me unconditionally

I can accept
help from
others

AUGUST 24

I am proud
of myself

AUGUST 25

Something new

Do something new today that you haven't done before.
Talk about your experience below.

I will not take other people's negativity

AUGUST 27

I will work smarter not harder

I choose happiness for my day

AUGUST 29

Journal

This simple practice improves mental clarity, offers the ability to see the big picture of our lives, and serves as a catalogue of every success we've ever had.

AUGUST 30

DECLARATION: I decree and declare that men and women in my bloodline will be overcomers! They will overcome any situation they face through grace and mercy of God, our Heavenly Father, and our Savior Jesus Christ!

AFFIRMATION: I am worthy of everything good in LIFE and deserve to be happy. I am intelligent and more than enough.

It was on Wednesday, June 15, 2016, in the sanctuary of New Beginnings. It incurred during a time of mourning. Three young women who wanted to talk to me asked me if I could stay after a dance rehearsal. Yes, of course, I can, I was so excited about ministering in dance on Father's Day. To my surprise, they asked me to find another ministry that fits my needs and where I was willing to serve and get along with others. This was my second time being asked to step down from the dance ministry. Now I was in awe because currently, I am experiencing what you call "CHURCH HURT," which is offense from the enemy to keep you from serving and going to the LORD'S' HOUSE! I served on several ministries, ushers, teen dance ministry leaders, women of purpose, business ministry, and greeter ministry, so finding a ministry fit was not an issue for me. The struggle I had was going back to New Beginnings after being humiliated twice. The pastor of the house was anointed and appointed, so I knew I was in the right place, but it was not my time and season to serve in ministry there.

I asked God every morning to create a clean heart in ME, and RENEW me a right spirit, feel me with the HOLY SPIRIT. God judges the heart, and the heart can be wicked or deceitful. The heart function is to pump BLOOD throughout the BODY. We are all parts of the BODY and have a different purpose. God judges the heart of man, and He is the only one that can turn the heart of men. I heard the spirit say, "They were wrong for that." Do not overcome evil for evil; you own nothing to man but love. Love covers a multitude of sins. Your labor will not go in vain. In 2017 my firstborn, his wife, and children moved to Sunny Florida, and then God said Candace you are next, get ready for your OVER-FLO-rida! For your OVERCOMING, you are an OVERCOMER! God was strategic and detailed as His lead me to Florida. In May 2018, I relocated to Tampa, Florida. On Mother's Day Sunday, May 13, I walked into my current church and seen praise dancers and looked up to God and said I think this is where I am supposed to be even though the word or message was not taught. It was the PRAISE DANCERS. Now I was let go on Father's Day and picked back up on Mother's Day!

So I want to encourage you, we have to stay humble. We have to change our mindset, watch our mouths. We need to ask God to fill us with the Holy Spirit to lead and guide us. We need to speak over our life and shift our atmosphere. WE shall prosper. God is with us...NOW BREATHE!

Candace Staples

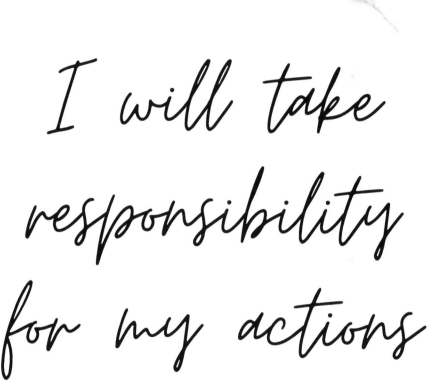

I will take
responsibility
for my actions

September

SEPTEMBER 1

DECLARATION: I decree and declare that I will love myself to life and teach everyone connected to me to do the same!

AFFIRMATION: I am intentional about loving myself to life, so that I will never hate myself to death, again!

In October of 2013, I found myself in a very dark place. I had experienced betrayal, loss, and recently divorced earlier that year. My life was spiraling out of control! I was mentally, physically, and spiritually ill. My mindset was so distorted that I fell into a deep depression, finding myself sitting in a dark bathroom for hours. So much so that my children, who were 10 and 19 at the time, had to check on me to make sure I was still alive. My health had become so bad that I couldn't hold down food, or anytime I would eat, it would cause me excruciating pain. I was going to church, but Sundays were where I was going through the motions, and then there were Sundays where I would give God a sacrifice of praise! I knew God for myself, but I had lost touch with him. I couldn't hear from him, and it was even hard to pray at times.

Fast forward to the next month, and my health begins to fail due to stress and worry. I remember it like it was yesterday, I hadn't been able to eat without being in pain all week long and hadn't been sleeping much due to the pain. My son was home from college, and I sent him to get me a plain baked potato, and I told him if I can't stomach that, I will go to the emergency room. Epic fail! I was in excruciating pain. My son rushed me to the hospital, and immediately, the doctor gave me medicine to relieve my discomfort. The medication was so powerful that it took the pain away instantly! I hadn't been asleep, so when I experienced relief, I immediately fell into a deep sleep! Moreover, when I think about it, it was God's way of putting me in a position to hear from him, with no distractions (I had so many of those).

As I was sleeping, I heard the voice of the Lord say, "are you done now? are you done fighting?" I replied, "yes, Lord, I'm tired!" I woke up to the doctor, shaking me and calling my name; I was just that asleep. I went home that night and realized that I had to do some things differently now! I had to trust God for real and love Paula back to life! How did I do that you ask? By taking it one DAE at a time!

Increase your prayer life, praise, and worship even when you don't feel like it. You will begin to see the distractions fall off, and your life will start to turn around. It worked for me, and two months later, I met my now-husband, who loves my life and is also my pastor. We have been married for six years, and we now have three beautiful children. I encourage you to love YOU enough to fight for your joy and peace of mind! It is
worth it!

Paula Watkins

SEPTEMBER 2

Goal Setting

Use today to set your goals for the year.
Be clear and specific with what you want to achieve.
Break the goal down into steps.
All the best in achieving your goals this year!

_____

_____

_____

_____

_____

_____

_____

_____

_____

_____

_____

_____

SEPTEMBER 3

I am a
winner!

SEPTEMBER 4

Prayer List

Take the time to pray for others today and
put their names below

SEPTEMBER 5

DECLARATION: I decree and declare that even during the storm, I am resilient and protected by God's grace.

AFFIRMATION: I am resilient in any season with His leading.

August 29th, 2005 was a day that completely changed my life. It was the day that I became jobless, homeless, carless, and lost my personal belongings, except for one duffle bag and one undergraduate degree. I was a twenty-something-year-old living in New Orleans, unsure about life, insecure about my future, heartbroken over a failed relationship; I was spiritually bankrupt. Ironically though, I had an innate sense of His presence in my life. A friend and I were planning to leave New Orleans for Atlanta for a previously arranged getaway over the Labor Day weekend to visit a mutual friend. After listening to the Mayor state on the local news that this storm would be catastrophic and may lead to deaths, I immediately walked outside, stood on my porch, and silently prayed. I could sense the "calm before the storm," and there was an eerie silence in the atmosphere. The humidity was so thick and unbearable, and then out of nowhere, a cold breeze passed over me, giving me chills, and I heard Him whisper "leave now."

I immediately called my friend to move up our time frame, and we headed to Atlanta. We hunkered down at my friend's house and watched the news display the storm's effects, and those three fateful words were heard and felt, leaving us devastated; "the levees broke." I knew instantly that my life had changed. It was then that my faith in God grew, and I began to see how he strategically used this storm to draw me closer to Him, teach me resiliency, and propel me forward. Hurricane Katrina became my catalyst for spiritual change and divine development, and although I was in the middle of the aftereffects of the storm, I had to envision myself on the other side of it.

I began to experience the grace of God in ways that I never knew existed. I asked Him for guidance and recognized that I needed to be obedient to His leading immediately. I then received a phone call from the CEO of a former employer in New York. She so graciously offered me a new position, an opportunity to rebuild, including assistance in finding a place to stay. In less than three weeks post-Katrina, God not only relocated me, but He provided me with everything that I lost and so much more. And when He whispered to me again to follow the call to apply to veterinary school, I obeyed and I found myself studying abroad on a little island in the Eastern Caribbean.

You have the privilege of feeling God in every detail of your life and know the direction He has for you is purpose driven. See that He is creating you to be resilient to withstand life's challenges. On the other side of the storm, you must be committed to serving Him faithfully with your words and life experience.

Natalie Ragland

SEPTEMBER 6

My business
income will
continue to
increase

Praise the LORD, my soul, and forget not all his benefits —who forgives all your sins and heals all your diseases, who redeems your life from the pit and crowns you with love and compassion.

Psalm 103:2-4

SEPTEMBER 8

Take the time to pray for others today and
put their names below

SEPTEMBER 9

The tools I
need are in
my possession

SEPTEMBER 10

DECLARATION: I decree and declare that the same mind that was in Christ Jesus resides in me.

AFFIRMATION: I am living with the mind of Christ.

When I was growing up, I saw a lot of witchcraft in my family. Someone that I know personally lost his mind and is still locked up in a mental facility today. This person has lived in a facility for the majority of his life. As a young woman, I knew it was wrong, and my heart went out to him. I knew that the devil had stripped him of his identity, and that bothered me so much where I knew I had to take action. I began to pray for him and cry out to God continually, and he has gotten a lot better. All glory to God!

There were times when the devil used to tell me I was going to lose my mind, I would never amount to anything, I was ugly, no one would ever want me, and I could go on and on. I refused to believe the lies of the enemy, and I chose to study the word for myself and see what God said about me. He said that I was fearfully and wonderfully made. I knew through prayer that He loved me, and He wanted me to take control of my thoughts.

Just because mental health issues run on both sides of my family didn't mean that it had to be my story. I began to meditate on His word both day and night. I found that through faith, my thoughts would change. I started to obtain the ammunition I needed to fight off the devil. I put on the mind of Christ! God hears us when we pray. All we have to do is take the time out to listen. I know He has kept me many days from doing things that I would regret.

If our ultimate goal is to be like Jesus Christ, we must think as He thought. While on this Christian journey, I learned that the Holy Spirit is our teacher. I could hear the Father saying, "Let this mind be in you, which was also in Christ Jesus. Let it be in you". When I truly embraced His word and studied and meditated on that scripture, my life changed. I would no longer settle! I no longer made crazy decisions based on my emotions.

We must begin to think as Christ thought. He wants our full attention indeed. Wherever He leads you, you must follow. This is where your strength and nourishment come from. The Lord has kept my mind, and if He did it for me, He can do it for you. The blessings have been so many I can't even keep track. Think of the impossible, because what's impossible with man is possible with God.

Markeeva Moore

I decree that anything is possible

I face the
day with
calm and
patience

My opinion
matters

SEPTEMBER 14

Encouragement

Take the time to encourage yourself today.
Write down your wins for the month!

My strength is greater than my struggle

I am fearless
with the Lord
on my side

SEPTEMBER 17

DECLARATION: I decree and declare that all generational curses are broken from my children in Jesus' Name!

AFFIRMATION: I am not bound by generational curses, past challenges or poor decisions; made by me.

I've faced many challenges throughout my life, but one that stuck the most was growing up in a single-parent home, which had its pros and cons. But one thing I never did was let it affect me in a way that caused me to act out in school or make negative lifestyle choices. I believe being raised in the church had a lot to do with being the strong-minded woman I am today. Although I remained in communication with my dad, the strength of the relationship wasn't there. From time to time, I would sit and think about how different it would have been with two parents in the home and how I wanted more positive memories as being daddy's little girl. I've learned that prayer is what keeps us sharp and makes us push harder. I vowed to myself that my children would not grow up the same way, and that curse of parents not living in the same home ended with me.

Affirmations and declarations were not used regularly around me while growing up, I seemed to hear more negativity than positivity about how life was and how not to end up. It wasn't until I became grown and started interacting with individuals who found their purpose and presented opportunities for me to be a part of a movement that brought me closer to God. I compiled a list of affirmations that help me with past and current challenges that I read daily. From time to time, I sit down with my children, explain to them things they may not understand, or why things happen when you don't keep or have prayer in your life. I say the following prayer to keep constant covering over my family and you can use it to. Repeat after me, Dear Heavenly Father, I rebuke patterns of sin that has trickled down from my family from generation to generation.

I rebuke teen pregnancy, addiction, gossip, laziness, depression, suicidal thoughts, bitterness, unforgiveness, jealousy, financial hardship, homosexuality, and any other sinful spirits that are not of you God. I plead the blood of Jesus and declare that the chains are broken, and curses are lifted. My entire family belongs to Christ, and no generational curses will tear us down or have power over our lives. In Jesus Name we pray, Amen!

You must pray with your children and expose them to God's word and let them know that the devil comes to cause destruction and disappointment, but God has come that we would have life and have it more abundantly.

LaQuita Hogan

But he said to me, "My grace is sufficient for you, for my power is made perfect in weakness." Therefore I will boast all the more gladly of my weaknesses, so that the power of Christ may rest upon me.

2 Corinthians 12:9

I was not
made
to give up

I declare that
I have the
power to
change my
story

SEPTEMBER 21

DECLARATION: I decree and declare that I embody a Godly spirit of power, strength, and self-discipline over my body, finances, and thoughts.

AFFIRMATION: I am fearless, loved, and I will trust the dreams God has planted in my heart.

Every summer granny would have all of her great-nieces and nephews visit so the older kids could help watch the younger ones. I can recall, one summer in 1987, being sexually abused by one of the older kids. I did not understand why, but when he told me that I was "pretty," it seemed right. That moment shaped the life that I would eventually live. The older I got, the more sexually curious I became. At the age of 15, I became pregnant, which devastated my family. I ironically miscarried on Easter Sunday while at church. Were things different? Did I start changing what I was doing? No.

At the age of 18, I planned to have a child with someone I was dating. We weren't openly dating, but we planned to get pregnant. As soon as I told him we were pregnant, he asked me to get an abortion, and I agreed. I was too far along in the pregnancy, and couldn't have the procedure, so he left me. I immediately thought I wasn't good enough! My son was born prematurely and placed in intensive care before coming home on Thanksgiving Day, November 1999. While I was going through my pregnancy, I met another guy. We were getting married, and I wouldn't have to raise my son alone. I finally felt worthy again! We secretly married, and everything that had happened in the dark came to light. He was HIV positive, on the down-low, wanting to prove to his family that he wasn't gay. I was his pawn, or was I? Daily I recall hearing the words, "you're enough, you got this," and I started to believe them. Four months later, we were separated, and I was no longer taking his verbal or mental abuse.

As I transitioned to another military base, I met countless young women who encouraged me as a strong young mother. I finally got it when my son and I lived in Indiana, where we attended church regularly. I don't recall the day or the hour, but a young woman who was also a single mother shared her testimony. From that moment on, I was more than enough. No sickness, diseases, addictions, or pain. A year later, I was asked by some students of the Black Student Union to share my story. Only a few years older than those young women, who knew, my account would be the same I'm sharing with you.

This past February, I was asked to share some words of encouragement in a ceremony celebrating women. The fear of not being enough attempted to creep back in. After prayer, meditation, and realizing my words are valuable, I agreed. That moment wasn't just for those ladies in the room, but it was a reminder that I am still more than enough. I pray that as you read my words, you too realize that you are enough, not because I said so, but because God has brought you through some tough times, and you are still here on top.

Lakisha Shannon

SEPTEMBER 22

Prayer List

Take the time to pray for others today and put their
names below

I use my failures as a stepping stone

SEPTEMBER 24

I declare that though these times are difficult, they are only a short phase of life

SEPTEMBER 25

DECLARATION: I decree and declare that my prayers are fortified according to God's will, and I understand that God is sovereign.

AFFIRMATION: I am a mighty woman of God changed by prayer.

In 2013, My sister died unexpectedly. Then six months later, my mother died. It was Martin Luther King weekend when my sister called me and asked me when I was heading to her house for the holiday. She was expecting me to come, and Thursday evening, I got the call from my son that she was in ICU unresponsive. They said she had a massive heart attack, and it seemed like things just spiraled down. I am a retired ICU nurse, so I understood all the machines and all the beeps. When we got there, I saw her, and it was like that moment in time stood still. I remember saying to my husband, "I'm praying that she makes it after a massive heart attack." I purposed in my heart that if she does, I will stop and take care of her because previously she had taken care of so many people. She had taken care of my mother and her mother-in-law at the same time. And before that, her brother-in-law and one of the members in her church all died in her home.

Earlier that month, we talked about how happy she was to make her husband's annual schedule and confirm all of his commitments. He preached everywhere. She said, "Now I could go be with him from city to city." That was a disappointment because I know what she purposed in her heart, and it was all about the ministry. When I got to the room, I asked who had been there and where were the nurses. I found out the neurologist and cardiologist hadn't been there. I requested the nurses to call him, and they never did show. The hospital was an ICU, but not by definition, and I asked that she be transferred for delay of services. By the time she got transferred, she had a flat line in her brain, and her heart was still beating. As my older sister and I prayed for her by the bedside, she would move her eyebrows and make facial expressions.

Eventually, the Lord decided to take her, and I didn't agree with it. I wanted him to answer my prayer the way I wanted him to answer my prayer. Maybe that wasn't her prayer. As we were at the bedside, we knew through the spirit that she had decided to go to glory. Through her unexpected transition, the severe issues I've experienced in breast cancer and radiation were nothing compared to what I felt when she left. In this season of my life, things have changed. I should've told the Lord I was scared and that I didn't want her to die. I felt so alone because I had to advocate for her caregiving, and I also had to release her to God's care. That's what we need to do—advocate, release, and surrender.

Don't dictate to Him what you want to do. Go in prayer with a blank slate so God can write the instructions. Go empty so that He can fill you. Don't go in prayer with preconceived notions. Go before God boldly and blank because you recognize that He is sovereign.

Dorothea Taylor

SEPTEMBER 26

Something new

Do something new today that you haven't done before.
Talk about your experience below.

_____
_____
_____
_____
_____
_____
_____
_____
_____
_____
_____
_____
_____
_____
_____
_____
_____

I know my
worth

I choose to
think
positively

I declare that
I am
conquering my
obstacles

SEPTEMBER 30

Prayer List

Take the time to pray for others today and put their
names below

October

OCTOBER 1

Goal Setting

Use today to set your goals for the year.
Be clear and specific with what you want to achieve.
Break the goal down into steps.
All the best in achieving your goals this year!

_____

_____

_____

_____

_____

_____

_____

_____

_____

_____

_____

_____

_____

I am open and receptive to all of the wealth that life offers me

I can do it
no matter
how hard it
is

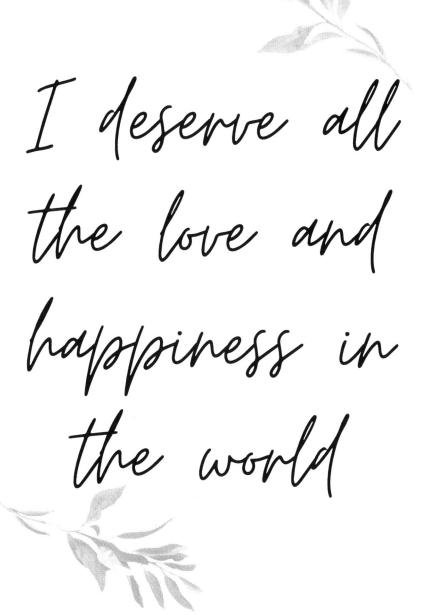

I deserve all
the love and
happiness in
the world

OCTOBER 5

Heart Check

Who do you need to forgive? Forgiveness is not for the other person. It is for you!

OCTOBER 6

DECLARATION: I decree and declare that I am a strong woman of God. He has created me for such a time as this.

AFFIRMATION: I am a strong woman and a woman of great purpose.

In October 2011, my first marriage took a turn for the worse. I never imagined I would have to deal with an affair, let alone domestic violence, which included mental, emotional, physical, and financial abuse. I felt unloved, rejected, abandoned, and mad. "How could this be my life?", I asked myself.

We had built a good life from the ground up. We had it all, or so I thought. What happened? What went wrong? All I kept asking myself was, what had I done to deserve this pain and hurt? I felt alone. I was so beat down mentally and emotionally from the negative words spoken over me. My mind was racing with thoughts. Embarrassed and ashamed, I was scared to tell our friends and family. I cried out to God many nights, hoping He would hear me and fix it somehow.

I felt a part of me had died that year. My dreams of a long-lasting marriage and raising our children in a loving and healthy home came to an end. I had a choice to make. I could stay in the marriage or put all my trust in God and step out on faith with my three children. I decided to leave a toxic and abusive marriage.

As I prepared months in advance, I prayed and asked God to open up for us, and He did! An apartment became available, and my safety plan was in place. I also went through my children's clothes, the clothes they wore often went in trash bags by the door as if I were going to drop them off to Goodwill. On October 14th, 2011, as I loaded the last bag and my children into the car. I felt like we were free, and that a blanket of peace was over us. I knew God was with us, and we were never alone.

Today I am in a happy, healthy, and loving marriage of three years to Brandon. We are blessed to have seven children between the two of us & one grandchild. Sometimes our journey is not always what we have planned. We must go through the fire and endure every trial and test in front of us, not just for ourselves but also for others. We may not know what tomorrow will bring, but one thing for sure, we will always have the victory through Christ Jesus.

Jennifer Ellington

OCTOBER 7

I have the
courage to
say no

I declare that I will be myself and let people see the real me

OCTOBER 9

Journal

This simple practice improves mental clarity, offers the ability to see the big picture of our lives, and serves as a catalogue of every success we've ever had.

I deserve a
time of rest

OCTOBER 11

I am open
and ready to
receive money

now

OCTOBER 12

DECLARATION: I decree and declare that I am WELL ABLE to carry out the plan God has ordained for my life.

AFFIRMATION: I am am favored by God. He downloads giftings and ideas that increase my wealth and business that bless my family for generations to come.

Being a single mom is tough. There are so many emotions and questions that encompass my title; guilt, shame, and feelings of defeat were my biggest. I always felt I fell short of some areas in children's lives, especially spiritually and financially. I tried to be the best mother, but I never measured up to the standard others put before me. I never knew how to ask for help or even if it was an option. So, I lived my life isolated even though I was surrounded by friends and love ones.

Living up to what others wanted me to be was killing me softly and slowly. I began to think I can't do this. I'm just not food at being a woman or a mother. I couldn't provide anything for myself or my children; food, shelter, or money. I remember praying, "God I am your child. I know this is not how I should be living." With tears streaming down my face, I said I give up. I can't do this and I'm sorry. It was as if God said, that's all I wanted. He began to take the heaviness away. He began to speak to me. He told me to read and write His word. His promises He made to me. The more I wrote, the more He revealed. It didn't happen all at once. Slowly He built my faith. He began to give me a new mind. He surrounded me with a new tribe of friends. They were women that would love me and sharpen me. They took the time to teach and encourage me. As I began to grow, new mentorship opportunities presented themselves. Mentor and counselors helped me to dig deeper and learn how to extract my purpose from the ugliness life had given me. I began to see things about womanhood and being a single mother differently. I continued to grow. I became better.

I once saw myself as worthless, but God loved me so much that He allowed me to gain the needed relationships that would eventually launch me into my purpose. I knew I couldn't keep the information to myself. I became who I once needed to be. I began to share with my friends, encouraging them to trust God and build onto their lives by living in purpose. My life was forever changed the day I truly surrendered to God. Whenever I feel shaken or insecure, I remember whom I belong to. I am the daughter of the Highest God. I am WELL ABLE to carry out the purpose and plan God has for me.

Vicki Legions

OCTOBER 13

Happiness is
a choice

OCTOBER 14

Encouragement

Take the time to encourage yourself today.
Write down your wins for the month!

_____
_____
_____
_____
_____
_____
_____
_____
_____
_____
_____
_____
_____
_____
_____

Have I not commanded you? Be strong and courageous. Do not be frightened, and do not be dismayed, for the Lord your God is with you wherever you go."

Joshua 1:9

OCTOBER 16

I focus on the positive

OCTOBER 17

DECLARATION: I decree and declare that I will use my words to strengthen other women continually.

AFFIRMATION: I am strengthened to encourage and impact other women's lives to believe in their possibilities.

The pain of divorce has its platform and the devastation of asking yourself numerous
questions but obtaining zero answers. January 2014 was the onset of the ending of a marriage, which I thought would last forever. I never thought that this journey was one in which I would experience again, but I did. I can remember when he and I were dating. Because we were both married before, we promised each other that divorce was not within the vocabulary of our relationship. Many things occurred within the twelve years prior to the decision. The one thing that did not happen was me now wanting to know if there was someone else lurking and waiting for my departure. Wondering whether I was as pretty enough, intelligent enough, or if this person now held the heart of an individual, which was once held by me!

I was so ashamed, hurt, and angry, and just mad because I no longer had the heart of the person who still had mine. My emotions were all over the place, longing for but having to release at the same time. My heart felt as if someone had taken a glass container and threw it against a wall, and all the broken pieces were my heart. As with any broken vessel, I asked myself, how do I pick up these pieces and try to put things together again. Moving on would be a challenge, but I also knew that staying would be a more significant challenge. August 19, 2014, my daughter and I left Dallas Texas en route to Tampa, Fl., not knowing what lay ahead of us but knowing that my life would never be the same! My daughter became such a strong force within my life, always encouraging, reassuring, and keeping a box of tissues available to dry my daily tears; God's Grace and her strength were pivotal during that season of my life.

In October 2014, my daughter and I found the Greater Life Christian church, where God began to place other strong and encouraging women in my life and allow each day to continue to heal my brokenness. Not only did God began to heal my broken heart, but at the age of 55, I completed my Masters of Science Degree and began again to walk in my calling. As a teacher of God's Word, I continue to encourage other women, letting them know that each day faced is another day closer to your divine healing no matter what your circumstance or situation.

We are stronger than we know, and we can do all things through Christ who strengthens us. We can, and we will continue to encourage, love, and uplift each other with the strength which God has Graced each of us with.

Patricia Buckner

OCTOBER 18

DECLARATION: I decree and declare that as I live in God, my love grows more perfect.

AFFIRMATION: I am committed to creating a positive outcome out of every situated presented to me.

I have dealt with many situations in my life that caused me to take it "one DAE" at a time. One relationship, in particular, was my son's father. Being that I was born into a type of hurt that can take years of healing, I found myself always disappointed and trying to move on to the next relationship or project when I needed to learn how to deal with the hurt.

Six months pregnant with my 4th child, I was being punched like a man repeatedly in my face. I was even told I was going to a graveyard to get pistol-whipped. When in reality, I
was locked in a room with only water and bread for hours, dragged by my feet into my own home and beaten so bad with a high chair that it left me with a black eye, swollen temple and blood clots up and down my legs. I had no choice but to work so that I could pay bills. I remember being scared for my life and believing all the lies of being told, "I'm sorry" or "I will never do it again, please take me back" or "Nobody else is going to love you like me!" Well, it happened again, and again it got so bad some nights that I would call my mom to hear her voice just because I was living in fear knowing. It was from decisions that I made from the pain of daddy issues.

Sometimes, I even felt like I deserved it because of the choices I had made in the past. Yes, there were times I just wanted to kill myself because I didn't know how to fix what I had gotten myself into. I could not bring myself to church during that time because my dad was a member of over 40 years in the church organization. That sight would have that constant reminder of him not being here for me. I didn't know how to get through the pain of continually making the wrong decisions in men and friends to fill a void. I used to think. If I had my daddy, I would not have gone through so much hurt.

My decisions of searching for love to fill a void that only my daddy could fill cost me a lifetime of lessons that I can never get back. I stayed in that abusive relationship for about two years. I got help from a girlfriend who allowed me to stay with her until I had a plan to leave. I did just that, and so can you! Nineteen years later, I'm able to pray for him and co-parent our son. I've learned that because I had lacked love in areas that I had no control over, that it does not make me who I am. I have smiled through a lot of hurt and pain, knowing that I wasn't happy and that this 12-second smile would only be for a moment when trying to cover a lifetime of damage. I got through it, and so can you. Allow that healing to begin in you! Believe in yourself and don't rely on the promises of others to make you happy.

Latrice Bryant

I take responsibility for who I am

OCTOBER 20

Accountability

Who is in your circle? Accountability eliminates the time and effort you spend on distracting activities and other unproductive behavior.

OCTOBER 21

DECLARATION: I decree and declare that my family, my seed, and bloodline will fulfill the purpose and plan of God for our lives.

AFFIRMATION: I am victorious and can do all things through Christ who strengthens me.

It was October 1986; I was seven years into my Air Force career, with a family and learning how to stand as a Christian. I had just come back from shopping and lunch with some friends. The weather was great, it was a holiday, and it had been a great day. My life as I knew it was heading in the right direction, so I thought, then the bottom fell out. What do you do when life happens, and you experience a loss of a loved one (who you thought would always be there) and are left standing there empty? I can remember standing in my kitchen in base housing with my mind overrun with thoughts. I am a Christian. I go to church. I pay my tithes. I pray, and I am a good person, this should not be happening to me.

Now, I am questioning myself and God's love for me and dealing with feelings of anger, failure, disappointment, fear, hurt, and pain. At times, the pain was almost unbearable, and I felt like I was falling apart. To keep myself together, I found myself putting on an emotional mask, to function. The "everything is great" superwoman mask: and then in my private moments taking the mask off and returning to my true feelings of pain, disappointment, and tears. There were times when it was a fight to make it through the day. If it had not been for the Lord carrying me and the support, encouragement, and love of my family and close friends during that painful season in my life looking back now many years later, I don't believe I would be the woman I am today. Today I am strong, wise, confident, and victorious in Christ. Today when trouble comes, I no longer feel the need to cover up with a mask, I can cry out to God for His help and strength to get me through it. Praise be to God, if He did it for me, He can and will do it for you also. Even though loss is a painful process for anyone to go through, we can get through it with God's help, taking it day by day.

Victory is on the other side of our surrendering and trusting in Him. Life is not always easy; going through the process is not always comfortable, but in those uncomfortable, sometimes hard times, God stretches our faith to make us better. We can be assured that no matter what process we may currently face, that God is faithful, He loves us with an everlasting love and will never leave us. We can become the mighty women that God has called us to be. We are not defined by what happens in our life; we are who God says we are: His masterpiece! Whatever the process, we can be encouraged knowing that God is with us and "we win"!

Dorothy Pettigrew

OCTOBER 22

DECLARATION: I decree and declare that I am a survivor of the wrong kind of love.

AFFIRMATION: I am a Queen, and a Child of God who knows what love is and my purpose is to help others overcome and learn that abuse is not love.

I have overcome so many obstacles in my life, and I know now that only God could have gotten me through. I have been raped, molested, and abused. My mother passed away when I was 15. God has been speaking to me and put it on my heart to talk about when I was physically abused, and I believe that the reason is to help other women who have been in similar situations.

I survived abuse from 9 years old until my adulthood. First, I was often physically abused by a family member and later in life by my boyfriends. I kept choosing the wrong person, again and again. When my boyfriend began to abuse me physically, I immediately went back to what I experienced in my upbringing. Even though I suffered abuse as a child, I wanted to think that my family member still loved me. I wanted to be loved so badly that I accepted it from my boyfriend as a sign of love. My wakeup call was when it almost cost me my life. I started dating my boyfriend when I was 17, and almost every other week, I was hit or emotionally abused.

One day that I will never forget was when we were driving, and he had picked up some drugs and asked me to hold it. I said, "No." I was immediately punched in the face and dragged to the back of the car. Blood went everywhere. I blacked out from being choked, my body went limp, and I was dying. The Lord spoke to me and said, "Go. I will make a way of escape for you. I love you, my child." Soon after, he ended up going to prison for drug charges. That is when I made my move and left, never to return. The next relationship I was in, I ended up being also abused. The Lord had spoken to me again and said, "Enough is Enough." I fought back and let it be known, "You will not treat me this way if you love me." Since that day, I have never suffered physical abuse again. I realized that God showed His love to us by providing, showing compassion, and even sacrificing His own Son to die for us. That is the kind of love that everyone deserves. Love is kind, love is patient, and love certainly is not abuse.

Life is not perfect. I know that once I finally understood how God wants us to be loved, things changed for me. You, too, can experience His love. We are all made in God's image. We must love ourselves even when nobody else will. I have been through so much in life, and I know that I went through those things to help others. This abuse may have happened to you or someone you know. Trust that you, too, can overcome.

Nitisha Hunter

OCTOBER 23

DECLARATION: I decree and declare that the Lord is my strong habitation and my place of refuge.

AFFIRMATION: I am blessed and comforted on every side; shame is not my portion because I trust in the Lord!

In April of 2005, at the age of twenty-five, my life began to shatter into what felt like a million pieces. My marriage and relationship of ten years ended as my spouse had chosen to start a new life with someone else. As a result, I unexpectedly became a single mother and the sole provider for our three sons, who were ages eight, two, and four months during that time. After shockingly finding his new love interest in our home and discovering that he had packed my belongings and those of our kids, I felt as if I was in an episode of the Twilight Zone. My sons and I moved into my parents' home. We shared my former bedroom, which had been converted into a small home office space. The room was a tiny and tight space for the four of us. However, I was grateful and knew that I could count on it being a safe place to dwell. It was previously my bedroom from ages twelve to eighteen. During this time, my feelings consisted of anger, hurt, disappointment, shame, and even rage. I felt humiliated that after ten years, three children, and overcoming numerous obstacles together, that the man that I called my husband was now choosing someone else over our children and me. Throughout what had occurred and what was to come, my faith in Christ is what ultimately kept me strong.

Less than one month later, our new safe place started to come to a sad end. My parents had separated and were also moving towards divorce. At this point, the hurt and burden of loneliness cut deeper than anything that I had ever imagined. Although our lives were not perfect, my parents' home was my safest place. It felt as if I had lost nearly everything and everyone all at the same time. I had no money, husband, parents, or a place to call home. For the next several months, my sons and I slept on my grandmother's tile living room floor, taking it one day at a time. Despite these natural losses, I held on steadfastly to my faith. By the end of 2005, the Lord blessed us with a three-bedroom apartment, which felt like the top of the world to us. Jesus explained in Matthew 17:20 that even with the smallest amount of faith, nothing is impossible, even the greatest of life's challenges.

It was faith, fellowship, and forgiveness that helped me successfully move forward. I trusted the Lord, and I forgave those who disappointed me. When life brings extreme challenges, we must trust God, realizing that He is our source, our strength, and our safest place. Rough roads are not easy, yet they are well worth the learning, growing, and stretching as the Lord makes them smooth to pave the way for us. My sons are now young men, ages sixteen, eighteen, and twenty-four. They are well and thriving in life. Today I am healthy, whole, and accomplished! I am a mother, grandmother, educator, encourager, and wife. Today our home is led by a God-fearing man who adores our children and loves me just as Christ loves the church. Stay encouraged and know that the Lord's plans for your life are good!

Mikesha Williams

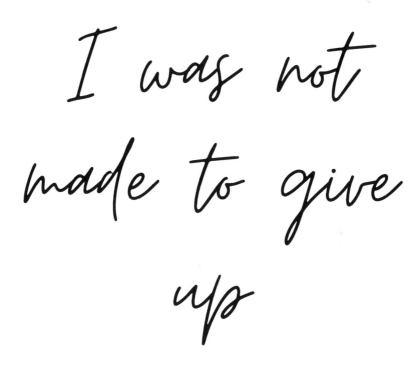

I was not made to give up

I'm brave enough to climb any mountain

I alone am enough. I have nothing to prove

OCTOBER 27

DECLARATION: I decree and declare that through God's love, grace, and glory, I can overcome any obstacle that stands in the way of me doing what God has purposed me to do.

AFFIRMATION: I am a woman who is created, protected, and loved by God because Jesus has already won the victory for me and I am committed to creating a positive outcome out of every situated presented to me.

We have all experienced challenges that we have had to overcome. Some of you may be facing a problem as you are reading this passage. I want to encourage you to keep pushing forward! No obstacle is insurmountable for our Father. And because you are His child, He has already given you every tool that you need to overcome any challenge set before you. One of the most reliable tools that you have is your faith. Your faith in God will give you the power to withstand and do things that you didn't think you were capable of doing. With robust and unwavering faith, God will provide you with peace in a chaotic environment.

Your faith can bring you through situations that you thought you could never get out of. Your faith in God can help you become the person you never imagined you could be. Your faith will help you open your eyes and see yourself as the woman God created to be loved, resilient, strong, bold, forgiven, and victorious! I want to encourage you, woman to woman not to give up, don't let adverse situations define who you are. Know that the power of the Holy Spirit lives in you, guiding you and helping you tap your God-given authority to overcome.

I have experienced and have had to overcome fear, rejection, hardship, and failure. There were times when I thought that I would have to settle for what was in front of me and be a victim of my circumstances. I believe that at some point or another, we have all been there. We were feeling boxed into our circumstances with no way out. I've had these experiences through financial hardships, job loss, betrayal, wrong decisions, and even suffering in situations that I did not create. I thought of giving up, I felt defeated, and I felt ashamed, but something in me wouldn't allow me to give up. I realized that I was getting in my way because I was trying to control and handle obstacles independent of God. It wasn't until I reached out to God, exercised my faith, and trusted Him to resolve my problems that I became an overcomer.

Everything is not going to be easy, and we're going to have some hard journeys and some steep mountains to climb. Just know that because you are God's child and that He sees you as an overcomer because you already are!

Sonya Sneed-Scott

OCTOBER 28

Encouragement

Take the time to encourage yourself today.
Write down your wins for the month!

_____

_____

_____

_____

_____

_____

_____

_____

_____

_____

_____

_____

_____

_____

_____

_____

OCTOBER 29

In all your ways acknowledge him, and he will make straight your paths.

Proverbs 3:6

I work with abundant enthusiasm and confidence

OCTOBER 31

I am stronger than anxiety and fear. Fear does not control me

November

NOVEMBER 1

Goal Setting

Use today to set your goals for the year.
Be clear and specific with what you want to achieve.
Break the goal down into steps.
All the best in achieving your goals this year!

_____

_____

_____

_____

_____

_____

_____

_____

_____

_____

_____

_____

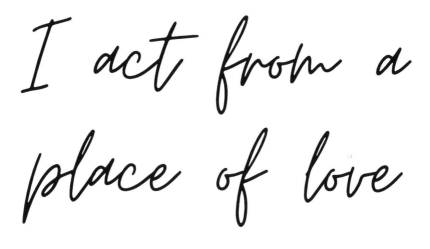

I act from a
place of love

NOVEMBER 3

DECLARATION: I decree and declare that my family will walk in boldness, having the assurance that they have been anointed and appointed for the journey.

AFFIRMATION: I am a powerful woman of God who learned through my grief that I am an Overcomer.

On February 29th, 1988, I gave birth to a beautiful baby boy. He was the joy of my life. I never knew love like this. Even though I was married, it was a different kind of love. I can't explain it. A year later, on July 19th, 1989, I gave birth to a daughter, who is the peace in my life. These two kids grew up together, being very close to each other. They always covered for each other even when it meant that both would suffer the consequences.

I received a call a few days after my son's 26 birthday, that would forever change my life. I was told, "Your son has been shot and killed." I remember crying profusely, saying, "No, God, not my baby." The pain was so intense. I was distraught. I kept thinking it's not true, it's not him, he's going to call me. I was in denial. Reality quickly set in, when a detective called to say the murderer would be having a bond hearing in 3 days if we wanted to appear. I knew I wanted to see this man. I wanted to know why he would kill my baby. I still could not understand how God would allow this to happen to me. I kept asking, "God, why, you knew the devil was going to kill my baby God, why God, why did you allow this?" I would have died for my child.

I was reluctant to be around people. I became very bitter and suffered from memory loss. I would go to the grocery store and could not remember what items I needed. I could not remember the security alarm code for the house. There were so many crying, sleepless, lonely nights. The grief was so unbearable. I just wanted to die. There was so much anxiety. No one could tell me how to get through this. I prayed every day, sometimes all day.

One day I screamed out to God. I began to feel as if someone was holding me; God's warmth was cradling me in his arms. I was finally able to take a breath and breathe. God is reminding you that He, too, had a son that died for you, and He knows the hurt and the pain that you are experiencing. You can take a breath and breathe. Each day, decree, meditate and pray to keep your mind stayed on God at all times so that you can now focus. Speak His word over your life. You will begin to smile again, which soon turns into laughter. I wanted to live again and trust God every day of my life, and from now on, you can trust God too.

Katrina Chamberlain

NOVEMBER 4

Take the time to pray for others today
and put their names below

_____

_____

_____

_____

_____

_____

_____

_____

_____

_____

_____

_____

_____

_____

NOVEMBER 5

DECLARATION: I decree and declare that my beauty is my blessing and my birthright!

AFFIRMATION: I am holy and set apart.

Living in a world that is hyper-focused on a woman's outer beauty can turn the most confident woman into a second-guessing self-loathing wilted soul. I know I was her! Though I was considered a beautiful child, and a gorgeous young woman so much that I modeled with Ebony Fashion Fair runway shows. I never quite grasped the real power, nature, and purpose of beauty. Not until I discovered that beauty, even my beauty, was a gift and responsibility. There are many stories in the Bible about beautiful women and their plight. Often, their plight came because of their beauty. Sarai's beauty caused her to be abducted by Pharaoh, and Abimelech threatened the life of her husband Abram. More often, their beauty served as a gift they could use to deliver themselves and others from their enemies. For example, Esther's exceptional beauty set her apart from other women. King Ahasuerus chose her because he "loved Esther more than all the women," she won grace and favor in his sight more than all the virgin. He set the royal crown on her head and made her queen (Esther 2:17).

Esther's beauty gave her favor. Her position ended up serving as a gift from God; that supernaturally set her apart to deliver God's people from annihilation. What a great gift and responsibility! What purpose does your beauty hold? How does your beauty serve God and others? I know. You probably don't feel that you are truly beautiful. But understand this truth: God "has made all things beautiful in its time". Therefore, if you are a living, breathing woman, you are "in your time" and possess beauty according to God's Word. Your beauty is distinct because it has its unique nature and power according to its divine purpose! Your beauty may be your superpower!

For years I squandered the power of my beauty trying to gain things in this world. To my shame, I was rarely satisfied or accepted. Instead, misuse of my beauty brought more despair. I was nearly 40 years old before I realized my gift of beauty was for God's glory and the advantage of others in my sphere of influence. A gift from God is an "endowment and a blessing." The recipient is not the focus of the present. The focus is on the people whom God will bless through the recipient's responsible stewardship of the gift. Today, I use my gift responsibly for the advancement of the kingdom of God. It aids me access spaces and ushers God's people into higher spheres of influence. The word of the Lord has come to you today to affirm that your beauty is real and complete! It is powerful, purposeful, for the glory of God, and the benefit of others. Walk in the power and blessing of your God-given beauty!

Declare with me today: My beauty is my blessing and my birthright! I will honor God with it, cultivate it, cherish it, protect it, embrace it, and use it to serve God and others. My beauty is holy and set apart, and God approves of it well! My beauty is for such a time as this!

Marguerite Isaac

NOVEMBER 6

My talents are unique to me

The fear of the Lord is the beginning of knowledge; fools despise wisdom and instruction.

Proverbs 1:7

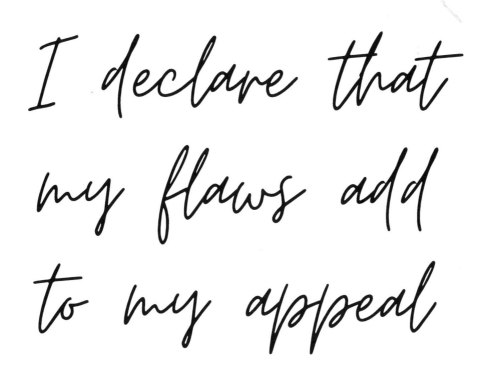

I declare that my flaws add to my appeal

NOVEMBER 9

Now to him who is able to do far more abundantly than all that we ask or think, according to the power at work within us.

Ephesians 3:20

NOVEMBER 10

DECLARATION: I decree and declare that I was chosen to endure.

AFFIRMATION: I am chosen to encourage and bring joy.

May 2019, I thought my life had taken a turn for the worse. I was diagnosed with Stage 3 breast cancer and had no idea what I was going to do. All my life my faith allowed me to speak joy into others. I encouraged everyone who crossed my path. I had unspeakable joy; I was born to laugh. My smile was my main accessory; I never left home without it. With my diagnosis, everything that I was used to doing for others I was now being tested to do for myself. My smile faded. How quickly a few words could change everything.

How would I tell my family, church and friends that I had cancer and was afraid? I could feel the tears wanting to flow while the rest of my body went numb. Then God reminded me that months prior, I told Him I wanted to know Him more and to be closer to Him. I came to understand that this was a part of my test of faith. Did I believe the very things I was preaching, encouraging, and telling others concerning God? I had nowhere to turn but to my faith. I was placed in an uncomfortable situation that was completely out of my control. My only assignment was to take a breath, smile again and TRUST - trust that God was who He said He was. Trust that He would Deliver, and trust that He was Able.

As my faith journey continued, there were so many nights of pain, feelings of loneliness, times I did not understand. I almost questioned, "Why me?" but knew it was all in God's plan. I was Broken to be Restored, molded and shaped by the Potter Himself. Everything in my life that had happened up to that point meant NOTHING. He had the power to GIVE and TAKE life and, for His Glory, He chose to spare mine. All I wanted was to LIVE, and it's what I do every day that I take a breath. Today, I breathe in thankfulness, grace, peace. My smile has returned, and I continue to encourage others during their times of testing.

We will be tested in this life. My journey proves that. But how we move through the test is what God is looking at. He wants our heart during the test. He wants us to rest in Him like I did when going through the cancer treatments. He allows us to endure humbling experiences so we can look at life from a different perspective. We can find Strength in ourselves that we never knew was there.

We were chosen in the womb and brought forth to give a message that GOD IS ABLE TO DO EXCEEDINGLY ABUNDANTLY ABOVE ALL THAT WE ASK OR THINK. I'm Healed, Delivered and Set FREE! He did it for me and He WILL do it for you!

Latasha McKnight

Be strong.
You never
know who
you are
inspiring

NOVEMBER 12

DECLARATION: I decree and declare that I will be who God created me to be, with no compromise or comparison, and I will no longer apologize for who I am and how I move in this world.

AFFIRMATION: I am bold, authentic, courageous, and unapologetic.

Most of us did not receive training in boldness. For the most part, we're raised to follow the script, color within the lines, and resist the urge to deviate from the mainstream. When faced with adversity, conformity, and shrinking are norms we rely upon as a weapon against the fear we feel. Then, fear starts driving the decisions we make—fear of rejection, fear of soaring too high, or fear of not being good enough. Anxiety, worry, fear! Can you relate? If I'm honest, fear shaped most of my life, and I watched it morph into vicious cycles of people-pleasing and endless quests for approval. This manifested into a history of bulimia, a series of bad relationships, the pursuit of a career I didn't want, and a pattern of stress-induced physical illness. Fear played a significant role in my diagnosis of depression and anxiety too. The constant negative self-talk while trying to live in conformity and perfection left me exhausted in mind, body, and soul.

As I grew in my relationship with God, I realized that my exhaustion was rooted in striving to be someone I wasn't created to be. Fear had trained me to play small and be quiet instead of using my voice to shift atmospheres and inspire personal transformation. Anxiety stole my authenticity and made me a fraud everywhere I went. It kept me apologizing for being who God created me to be rather than remaining true to who he said I was as he formed me in my mother's womb. Fear drove me to be passive-aggressive and an expert at hiding when God said that I am bold as a lion. I've learned that it takes an intentional commitment to God and a covenant agreement to make him the top priority and center of my life to combat fear.

To that, we must add consistent doses of therapy and connection to a loving and supportive tribe who holds us accountable to God's greatness. To be clear, this is daily work! Each day, we must decide to be bold and courageous by confronting fear and doing the things that God calls us to do even in the face of adversity. Each day, we must decide to get clearer on our divine identity and act accordingly! The only person God expects us to duplicate is Christ. Each day, we must decide to stop apologizing for being God's unique creation and for sharing our voice and gifts for his glory. It's daily work but let's do the work! We need YOU in this world! And you know what? We will not worry about how we will do it because we have Holy Spirit in us, and he gives us the power and divine enablement we need to do what we cannot do on our own.

Dr. Synetheia Newby

My reputation precedes me before I get there

I deserve to be fully loved

NOVEMBER 15

DECLARATION: I decree and declare that I will rise above every hindrance that would attempt to eradicate my impending victory over feelings of fear and inadequacy.

AFFIRMATION: I am more significant than any obstacle that I might because I am a King's daughter and the promise on my life must be fulfilled.

The year was 1991. I remember the feeling of the crisp winter air as it blew lightly against my face. We were gathered together for track and field practice. Gazing across the open infield, you could hear the rhythmic sound of spike donned feet traveling at lightning speed around the freshly resurfaced track. Our school was known for producing world-class sprinters. These ladies were phenomenal athletes, and they were varsity level competitors. They had years of experience and preparation behind them. I had only participated in 100-meter dashes in a middle school field day setting. In contrast, these ladies had stood on the podium to receive numerous medals for their performances, both individually and collectively.

I remember the fear that came over me when I received the news that I had been selected to train with the varsity girls, even though I was but a freshman. I was extremely excited, but I was equally as nervous. I knew there was much work to do if I wanted to be successful. Our coach instilled the importance of persistence and preparation. There were days that we pushed our bodies to the maximum limits allowed by nature to receive the ultimate reward. It did not matter if we were first-place finishers or the last to reach the finish line; we were winners because we did not give in. But truth be told, we wanted the victory every time our spikes hit the track. I remember long days of running miles and miles throughout the neighborhood, with the coach following closely behind in his minivan. He would scream instructions and helped us with pacing and breathing. During the summertime, while our friends enjoyed the summer break, we were required to run three miles daily on the same rigorous cross-country course, which is where prize-winning horse races ran. There were times that I wanted to give up and walk away from the prize. But my coach kept pushing me. He reminded me that sometimes you must continue to press individually so that you can win collectively. At first, I did not fully understand. But as the individual members of our 100-meter relay team continued to work towards one common goal, we quickly realized that we were responsible for our team's collective success.

To complete our race, we had to pass the baton without dropping it along the way. This required consistent preparation, discipline, encouragement amongst our peers, and, most all, perfect timing. We each had to focus on doing our part to obtain the ultimate victory. Sometimes we are so focused on the ability of others in the same race, that we lose sight of our God-given talents. We must remember that someone's destiny is tied to our willingness to move forward. The victory is ours for the taking. Keep pressing through the difficult times and tough terrain. Success consists of ups and downs. Embrace the entire journey.

Tanya Thompson

NOVEMBER 16

Encouragement

Take the time to encourage yourself today.
Write down your wins for the month!

My life is
a message to
the world

NOVEMBER 18

DECLARATION: I decree and declare that I am an overcomer of anything I have endured, no matter the obstacle, the strain, the struggle; I will continue to inspire and encourage others to walk boldly in faith.

AFFIRMATION: I am a strong woman who continues to pray and stay faithful to God's promises.

Have you ever experienced that breaking point where it felt like everything was against you, and you did not know where to turn? For me, it was December 2012. I had dealt with a broken relationship. I met a man whom I thought would change my life. I felt loved, wanted, respected, and safe. I was wrong. You see, May 2014, a year and a half later, I would end up in the worst place, mentally, emotionally, and physically. I found out he had cheated and had been manipulating me for most of our relationship. I felt lost and emotionally bruised. I prayed to God for an answer, and he said to me, "I needed your attention." I started going back to church and focusing on building my relationship with God as everything else I had tried on my own had failed miserably. You see, I knew of God but did not have that relationship with God. I had been praying all those years, and it seemed like God was ignoring me.

The breakup shifted me into unfamiliar territory. I found a new church home where I learned more about having a faith walk and finding my purpose. Shortly after that, I realized that God was positioning me to start my nonprofit organization, which advocates for domestic violence victims. I needed to experience the abuse as a child. Then in my relationships, I needed to deal with manipulative men in order to gain the knowledge, grow the strength, and build the faith needed to run this organization. Yet I continued to struggle with my faith because God was asking me to walk away from my career after 20 years and a salary of over eighty grand a year.

I was single with no children, living with no outstanding debt, and I was balling. I felt as if my career was my provider. A few years went by, and I continued to disobey God's calling, my faith wavered, I continued to go to church, tithe, and serve, but I still battled with my faith daily. God was so patient. In September 2015, I got promoted to an extra dangerous position that I never applied for. I asked God to block the position if it was not something he had in His will for my life. Well, two days later, I got the call stating I got the position. Six months later, I took early retirement after praying for guidance. You see, God will place us in uncomfortable situations to force us to move when given an assignment.

How many of us have questioned God's word or will for our lives? If we can gain just a mustard seed amount of faith, we can move mountains. I encourage you to hold on to God's word. In Jeremiah 29:11, He knows the plans He has for us, to prosper us and not harm us, to give us hope and a future. I challenge you to stand firm in his word.

Lorrie Shepherd

NOVEMBER 19

I am an inspiration to others

I am made
with greatness

The fire of
God burns
within me

NOVEMBER 22

Something new

Do something new today that you haven't done before.
Talk about your experience below.

I am a new creation in Christ

I deserve time
to recharge

My mind is
renewed

NOVEMBER 26

DECLARATION: I decree and declare that my children down to the 4th generation will be oaks of righteousness, strong, lofty, and magnificent. We will stand for God, walk-in integrity, and have a Spirit of Excellence that HE may be glorified forever!

AFFIRMATION: I am the right person with the right gifts, in the right place, at the right time!

My first-grade teacher, Sister Hermon Joseph, posted a long white sheet of paper with numbers across the green chalkboard. She said, "each number represents your crayon's color that I will pass out to you. When I call your name and number, go to the board and color in your portion of the picture". Every day at art time, Sister Hermon Joseph would go into the closet and come back with a big cigar box filled with many colored crayons, and we would choose our favorite color. I always chose red because it was my favorite color. If anyone chose red, I would trade with them. After a while, no one would choose red. But today, she did not give us that option. Instead, she went into the closet, walked around the room, reached in the box, and gave us a crayon. When she got to me, she reached in the box and put a GREEN crayon in front of me. GREEN! There must have been a mistake.

She knew my favorite color was red. I did not like green; I liked red! As I began to ask if anyone wanted to trade, she said, "no trading, all colors are beautiful." She then said, "children, you will proceed to the board in alphabetical order by your FIRST name." My name is Venetia, and that meant I was going to be last! Not only do I have a green crayon that I do not like, but I am going to be last. Besides, who colors with green? I would have even considered blue or purple, but not green! One by one, each kid was up coloring, and the picture was coming together. By the time it was my turn, the kids were yelling for me to run up to complete the picture. The first item I chose to color looked different with only two colors of red and yellow but, as I began to add my green, the shape started to come. When I had finished, the picture was a parrot! Next, I added my color green to the head of a duck.

As I moved to the next part of the paper, the kids were now standing, clapping, and yelling for me to color quickly. I then took my green crayon and colored leaves, a frog, top of trees, and lastly, I put my color, GREEN, in the rainbow! The picture was now complete. As the cheers from my classmates grew louder and louder, for the first time, I was glad to have been given the color, green. I felt needed and essential that day.

The lesson I learned: I am needed, I am important, and the picture is complete with me. I will never let anyone disregard me. We all are different, but our purpose is essential. I encourage you to be proud of who you are as a beautiful, resilient, secure, and unique you!

Venetia Waters

I am a
mountain
mover

NOVEMBER 28

Journal

This simple practice improves mental clarity, offers the ability to see the big picture of our lives, and serves as a catalogue of every success we've ever had.

_____

_____

_____

_____

_____

_____

_____

_____

_____

_____

_____

_____

_____

_____

I am a stronghold breaker

My past has shaped me into something wonderful

December

DECEMBER 1

DECLARATION: I decree and declare I am stepping into God's Glory as his Foot Soldier.

AFFIRMATION: I am no longer allowing my past obstacles to become a barrier between God and my blessings.

At times you believe or want to think you are making the right decision, especially when it comes to marriage. In 1985, three months after my baby girl was born, I began to notice red flags. I tried to ignore the red flags, but they screamed at me, so I could no longer ignore them. The red flags were infidelity, gambling, drugs, and emotional abuse. He was not putting the marriage first, and I could no longer be the receiver. Sometimes we become so clouded by the flesh that we are led by the sentiments of love but not what God calls us to do. I became angry, ashamed, and overwhelmed. I felt I was losing myself, and I was in pain. I felt I let God down. I didn't have resources available, and I was overwhelmed by the legal aspects of ending my marriage. I prayed not to allow my brokenness to delay my destiny God had for me. There I was with clarity, having to make a difficult decision. I never was so clear about a decision to move on and let go.

At times I wasn't sure because all I wanted was that fairytale to be married forever. I moved forward and filed for divorce. Here I was with a baby and unclear what would be for us as a family. I did know that through all my struggles, God has never left my side; he has always walked with me, despite me not being clear. I began to look at what I needed to do to survive. First, I had to pray and become God's Foot Soldier. Secondly, I had to take the gifts that God gave me and put them into action. I did just that I applied for a job. Finally, I secured daycare for my baby. I have learned when God orders your steps; it is up to you to follow. We may not be ready, or we may not understand the reasons at that time. I prayed to God to come into my presence and guide me. He did. He gave me oxygen to my soul. I did not look back, although it was so overwhelming. It all seemed to be a blur. As I was growing in wisdom, I became stable and focused on God's walk. All the special memories seemed to be blurred, but not the way my baby called me "Ma Mia." I often asked, "Why Me?" I continued to keep God as my center brought me peace and the will to carry on.

When the divorce became final, I cried like a baby because it seemed like a death ending a relationship that was to be forever. I experienced an unexplainable sadness. I began to walk in God's light and manifest his abundant blessings. I know when darkness enters our beings, we should surround ourselves with one another, so we could draw strength from one another and serve one another. So, we can be transformed by the reflection of God's Glory! Our burdens are what strengthen us and prepare us for our faith journey and allow us to have a purpose and grow into the women God destined us to be! Seeing God in our mirror is our perseverance!

Robbin Johnson

DECEMBER 2

DECLARATION: I decree and declare that I break the generational curse of addiction and family unit breakdown; through the power Christ has in my life.

AFFIRMATION: I am cared for and carried by God, developing every day into the woman that God has predestined me to become.

Has there ever been a time in your life you felt uncared for? My early life experiences were rooted in domestic violence, abandonment, and sexual molestation. Struggles with addiction influenced the lives and hearts of my loved ones contributing to the breakdown of the family unit, and as a result, I spent a lot of time alone, and deep down, I felt like no one cared for me. I buried my feelings and chose to be secure in myself and tried to care for myself through my works and was unaware that I had a God who cared for me, I contributed to many messes through my decisions. While everything looked beautiful on the outside, it was a constant struggle with identity, struggles with my sexuality, shame, self-worth, anger, and depression. I blocked myself from people and I avoided close relationships with people.

One day, I had a dream of a particular co-worker. At that time, I knew very little about this co-worker personally. It was December 2015. Our company was closing down in hopes of picking up another contract. It was the very end of the day, and I wasn't sure if I would cross paths with her again. I was hesitant, but I obeyed the prompting within and shared the dream of her praying. She didn't say much, but we kept in contact. I found out that someone I worked with would become someone who cared for me. Through God working in her and through her, she was able to minister to my life. She created a safe place for me to open up and encouraged me to seek healing and guidance on how to do so. It felt like she pulled my covers off at times, and I wanted to disappear. Through that, I learned to be authentic, and if I wanted to grow in God, I could not hide. God placed people filled with his spirit to care for others through ministry, and I chose to follow. I began a more rooted, non-superficial, personal relationship with God, and he began to show me the areas in my life where I was hurting and gave me the keys to free myself from my prison. One of the first keys I received was the key to Forgiveness. I was able to forgive others and not harbor resentment in my life for what others did to me or didn't do for me.

I began to recognize myself as cared for by God. I now desire to serve others and love people more and seek relationships and friendships with others. I am no longer in hiding, and my marriage is now flourishing. I am a Godly wife and mother to my children. I am free from depression, and I have healthy work relationships. We must speak up for ourselves and create boundaries. I have a fire to pursue the things of God and help others, just like many of you do. I have forgiven everyone, even those who have hurt me, and I have a desire to show them the love of God. God is our Healer, and He never forsakes or abandons us. You are cared for by God.

Angelica LaGuerre

DECEMBER 3

Goal Setting

Use today to set your goals for the year.
Be clear and specific with what you want to achieve.
Break the goal down into steps.
All the best in achieving your goals this year!

_____

_____

_____

_____

_____

_____

_____

_____

_____

_____

_____

_____

DECEMBER 4

DECLARATION: I decree and declare that everything I do and everyone connected to me is important, relevant, useful, and necessary because the Almighty God says so.

AFFIRMATION: I am important, relevant, useful, and necessary!

The day that my mom told me that someone molested my sister when she was a young girl is a day that I will never forget. I remember it as if it had just happened yesterday. It was June 1991, and I was 12 years old. I came in from school, and my mom was home. She usually didn't get in until the evening. I went into the living room where my mom and sister were, and as soon as I walked in, I could feel something was wrong. You could see in my mother's eyes whatever she was getting ready to say was not going to be good.

I thought she was about to tell me that someone passed away, or maybe I was in trouble (even though I didn't do anything wrong). I had no thought that she was going to tell me that someone close to me had hurt my sister, but to my surprise, she did. At that moment, I became filled with guilt. I knew it was not my fault, but for some reason, I took ownership. I remember standing there with tears in my eyes, feeling angry and guilty.

Even though my mom repeatedly said it was not my fault, I couldn't shake that guilt. From that moment on into adulthood, I developed a character where if there were a chance at any time, I would find myself having to feel guilty; I was going to avoid that feeling. Through time, I focused on making sure that I didn't have to feel guilty; I didn't realize that I was diminishing my self-worth and importance in the process.
I convinced myself as long as everyone was good, then I was fulfilled even if I am not able to achieve what I set out to do it was because it's not about me. I convinced myself that God's only purpose for my life was to meet the needs of others. I convinced myself that if I had to place my obligations to the side, they were not relevant at that time. In telling myself this, I forgot that God had put so much more in me, and I had forgotten about how God had so much more waiting for me.

Has there been a time in your life where you always told yourself it's not about me? Has there been a time in your life where you knew that God's purpose was more than receiving the fulfillment from meeting the needs of others? Well, let me tell you this WE GOT THIS! Being fulfilled is not about us, but instead, it's about God. Everything we do should be done unto God and not unto man.

Lasaraha Bell

I declare the failure doesn't come from falling down. Failure comes from not getting up

DECEMBER 6

Prayer List

Take the time to pray for others today and
put their names below

_____

_____

_____

_____

_____

_____

_____

_____

_____

_____

_____

_____

_____

_____

_____

Don't start because it's easy, start because it's worth trying

DECEMBER 8

Journal

This simple practice improves mental clarity, offers the ability to see the big picture of our lives, and serves as a catalogue of every success we've ever had.

DECEMBER 9

DECLARATION: I decree and declare that I am an overcomer, a devout woman of faith who is destined to live on the larger side of life.

AFFIRMATION: I am more than a conqueror through Him Who loves me, despite my share of past hardships, tragedies, and afflictions.

In February 2013, God revealed just how much of a strong woman I am, mainly after I laid my infant son to rest. I realized that real battle unfolded because God gave me the strength and courage to overcome and, most importantly, to encourage others through my life-altering experience. I recall having spent a considerable amount of time with God, during which I grasped a real sense of guidance on how to navigate this dreaded season while diligently being healthy for my daughters. I realized my desire to lead by example had subsequently taken a toll on me, especially when I witnessed my babies often comforting and reminding me that all things would work together for good. We as women must remember to make it a point to find a way to smile every day or, as I would often suggest to others, to "smile regardless." Just as I would channel my energy toward getting closer to God, which gave way to discovering my passion for baking, we all must allow alone time with God to lead us to things that will help guide us to our destiny.

By the grace of God, my baking business has enjoyed considerable success since the beginning. God impressed it upon my heart to often offer words to encourage mothers who likewise had to bear the pain of infant loss. At times, I wondered how I would be able to help someone else when truth be told; I was still grieving. One day, I was contacted by a high school classmate during a rather dark season in her life, which mirrored my son's death. From that point, God infused me with the Holy Spirit's light to share some wise counsel and encouragement with her and other women. Understand ladies that tough times will inevitably surface, but in those times, we will possess a peace that surpasses understanding. For us, as women, those are the times to become more dependent on God because we serve a Savior Who pledged never to leave nor forsake us.

We must believe that He will provide for us a way of escape. I encourage you to view every trail and every form of adversity from God's perspective, for the Father is only preparing us for more significant platforms by which to share our testimonies. Understand there is no testimony without a test, and that every test is God's platform by which He will bless us. Understand every obstacle we endure is a strategic setup for God to thrust us ever-so-closely toward our destiny. Stay in faith, realizing beyond a shadow of a doubt that God will make all things new. And that, women of God, is my prayer for you.

Latambria Johnson

I am brave, bold and beautiful

I declare that when God steps in, miracles happen

DECEMBER 12

Prayer List

Take the time to pray for others today and put their names below

_____
_____
_____
_____
_____
_____
_____
_____
_____
_____
_____
_____
_____
_____
_____
_____
_____
_____

DECEMBER 13

DECLARATION: I decree and declare that our family will break the generational curse of negative patterns and thoughts.

AFFIRMATION: I am responsible for birthing my destiny.

For 18 years, I grew up in a rough area, where your dreams had to be bigger than your reality to get out. I believed I would not amount to anything, because that's what I kept hearing. I continued to tell myself, "I'm not worthy of leaving this lifestyle, why would it happen to me?". I had always wanted more in life, but negative thoughts still blocked my blessings from coming. After getting pregnant at 15, I got held back in the 9th grade. The stigma with adolescent pregnancy came with the idea that adolescents would drop out of high school, and due to a lack of skills, they were unable to get a well-paying job. Thankfully, God blessed me with my mother. She watched my daughter daily. I had to forget about having fun with friends, going out, or just enjoying my youth. I got married at 18 years old, had a second child at 18, and a third at age 21. I married, divorced, and now with three kids to raise on my own.

In 2008, when my children were 6, 3, and 6 months, I decided to join the United States Air Force. Little did I know that I didn't make enough money to bring them with me. I cried almost every night for months. I felt like a failure; I wondered, "what would be the point of changing my life if I couldn't bring my kids with me?" I lost faith; I was angry; I was going through a divorce. I started to feel that negative energy coming back. My spirits were low, but this time instead of focusing on my challenges, I started to focus on what I had accomplished and how I can continue to use my time away from my kids as motivation to work harder. I received two AS degrees, a BA in Psychology, and currently halfway through with my Double Major MBA. I wanted to make sure that my kids would be proud of me and my accomplishments. Later on, my life changed when I allowed my now spouse to enter my life; we purchased our first home and completed our family with our fourth child.

The advice I give my kids daily is always to work hard, never give up, and dream big. I don't want them to be like me; I want them to be better than me. Generational curses can only exist if we allow our dysfunctions to be hereditary and not situational. Prove to yourself that you are worthy. You may lose a few battles, but you will not lose the fight. We tear ourselves down with our negative thoughts; we miss opportunities, we lose focus on our purpose. We even self sabotage our lives and question what we can accomplish. It becomes even more challenging when others test or doubt what we are capable of. I am living proof that although there are struggles, negative thoughts, and doubters, the fight will lead us to a successful path when we show perseverance, strength, and faith that all things happen to lead us to where we need to be.

Dorixa James

DECEMBER 14

DECLARATION: I decree and declare that the breath of God, the Ruach of God, fills my lungs and atmosphere.

AFFIRMATION: I am calm, and I do not panic, knowing that I am yielded and led by the Holy Spirit; therefore, anxiety, panic, nor stress can control me.

It was 11 o'clock on a crisp, sunny morning. Yet, I find myself sitting in the middle of my bed, crying, "Father, Father, help me!" I had come to know this type of prayer. I call this a "desperate" prayer that had become so familiar to me over 2 ½ years. My family was in a time of perpetual trials. One day, my husband shared that he didn't feel well. He stood up from our bed and proceeded to walk into our open bathroom. While standing at the sink, I noticed that he was sweating profusely. He continued to splash water on his face and walked into the toilet room. After he was there for about 5 minutes, I heard a loud "ting." This sound would be the beginning of this trial. I ran into the toilet room only to find him helpless and stretched out in a not so comfortable position. He had fainted in the restroom. I remember arriving at the hospital frantic. I was praying but afraid and unsure of his status.

As I stood in the ER bay, I remember thinking, "this is no place I want to be." What I didn't know at that time was that I would have many visits to this bay. Your life can indeed change instantly. I found myself responsible for and having to take on all the responsibilities of our household, our children, our business, and ministry responsibilities. My days would be overwhelmed by guilt. It was undoubtedly an unexpected shift. Then, as I was driving down the road, my heart began to race, I began to sweat, there was a pain in my back, my vision blurred, and I COULD NOT BREATHE. I quickly pulled over, called 911, and told them I had a heart attack. After many tests, the EMT arrived, and after a couple of nights' stay, I left the hospital. The doctors told me that I was in excellent health. I couldn't believe it. As the days went on, I didn't know what was happening. I knew I couldn't breathe, and there was no medical explanation. I was tired, and I didn't know how I could go on. Sitting in the middle of my bed, I begin to cry out, with tears streaming down my face, I begin to say, "Father, Father, Help Me." The Holy Spirit whispered, "Rest in my bosom" & "It tried to knock the breath out of you, but I wouldn't let it." In those moments, I found new strength and rest.

I want to encourage you today. If you are currently in a place thinking, "this is no place I want to be," in that place where it seems like you can't breathe, it seems like the pressures of life are overwhelming you, you are not alone.

Life's situations may have come to restrict your breath, but the Holy Spirit is your comforter, and God is your shield. You will not lose your breath, and you will make it through this trial.

Andrea Jackson

DECEMBER 15

Journal

This simple practice improves mental clarity, offers the ability to see the big picture of our lives, and serves as a catalogue of every success we've ever had.

_____

_____

_____

_____

_____

_____

_____

_____

_____

_____

_____

_____

_____

_____

<u>DECEMBER 16</u>

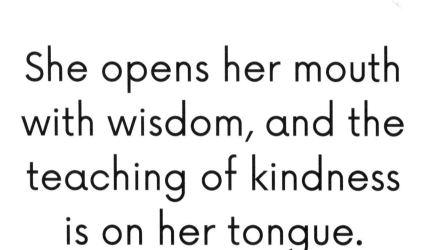

She opens her mouth with wisdom, and the teaching of kindness is on her tongue.

Proverbs 31:26

I have enough self-worth to not seek revenge

DECEMBER 18

DECLARATION: I decree and declare that I no longer live in fear, and I no longer need others' approval.

AFFIRMATION: I am a courageous and confident daughter of God, and I am secure in God's love for me.

God delivered me from low self-esteem and gave me the courage to walk away from a toxic marriage. During my second year of college, I married a Christian guy I had known for a little over a year. We bonded over these experiences and insisted that we would not repeat the cycle. Looking back at our conversations, we bonded over our wounds and not God's purpose. Plus dealing with the struggle of staying celibate, I figured the best thing to do was to "marry instead of burn," as the old folks say. But I should have paid attention to the signs.

Yield signs to slow down and stop signs to stop me in my tracks, but I kept going. I noticed how he would blow up after a disagreement with me, his friends, and his family members. Sometimes, he would slam doors and punch holes in walls. After years of marriage, the anger issues didn't go away; it just got worse. He started smoking, drinking, and hanging out late with friends. This behavior only added to my shame, but because of my pride, there was no going back. I didn't want to divorce because I didn't want to prove others right, and I tried to keep up appearances.

When I felt like things were too much, I was told to keep praying, and things would change. Things never changed, and I began to hate my life. One morning, I found my husband passed out on the floor. I remember my daughter and son asking me what's wrong with daddy. I could see their fear and tears running down their cheeks. I reassured them that their dad was going to be okay and send them away. At that moment, I looked at myself in the mirror for the first time and saw the years of weight gain brought on by stress. I also started thinking about the example I was setting for my daughter. She was getting older, and I could no longer hide his alcoholism. I decided to leave my husband and file for divorce. I could no longer allow myself or my kids to stay in that environment. I was fearful and ashamed, but God gave me the courage to move forward despite the church folk talk and the fear of disappointing others.

God gave me the courage to see that I only needed to please Him, and this situation wasn't His plan for my life. This was my life, and I had to decide to take care of my children and me. I want to encourage you to be secure in God and know that He is the only one you need to please. Remind yourself that you are a bold woman walking in purpose and giving others the courage to stand up for themselves and live for God alone.

Kimberly Sinclair

Don't stop because it's hard, stop because you've tried your best

DECEMBER 20

Journal

This simple practice improves mental clarity, offers the ability to see the big picture of our lives, and serves as a catalogue of every success we've ever had.

DECEMBER 21

DECLARATION: I decree and declare that in every trial I went through, every test placed in front of me and all future endeavors are necessary for my next level.

AFFIRMATION: I am a masterpiece of refined, sparkling, shining gold that was created under fire.

For ten years, I struggled with financial stability. During those years, I had to work several jobs, overtime hours, all while being a single mother. Life seemed so unfair, and it seemed that everyone else was excelling and financially able to care for their families, and I could not. I felt inadequate, alone, frustrated, and tired of having to make things happen to take care of my children. There were times that I questioned the assignment God had for me. "God, did you have me to go through all of this schooling to obtain a degree, and I am still struggling to care for my children? Every-day, I am encouraging, inspiring, and teaching your people, only to come home, continuing to wonder, when is my breakthrough coming." I knew that God was going to take care of me like He always had, but I am still human. Often, I cried, I prayed, I wrote, looking for relief, financially, emotionally, and physically.

In 2018 and 2019, I began to ask God what am I missing? I trust you. I know that you have anointed me to do what I am doing, but what else am I missing? I begin learning about the power of manifestation. I started trusting my spirit more and continuing to be obedient to the things that God was commanding me to do. God then showed me that every opportunity I had received until that time was still one level higher than the one before. He showed me that at each level, there was a lesson to be learned, some people I needed to meet, and an increase of faith I needed to have to grow closer to Him.

We have to continue to increase our faith and stay steadfast in our connection to the source of power; prayer, meditation, learning the Word of God, and staying connected to other spiritual uplifting people. Stay engaged to things and people that feed you spiritual, also those things that challenge us and encourage us to do better. Just because our situations and circumstances do not look the way we think it should, does not mean that God's promises to us have changed. His purpose for life never changes, although we cannot see or understand the route, He chooses to take us through. No matter what life throws your way, always keep your hands in God's hands.

No matter what trials and tribulations come your way, if we stay anchored in God's promises and trust what he tells us, He will bring us out on the other side. He never promised us that things would be easy, but He did tell us that all things are possible.

Lashica Charley

DECEMBER 22

My life is
worth it

DECEMBER 23

Prayer List

Take the time to pray for others today and
put their names below

_____

_____

_____

_____

_____

_____

_____

_____

_____

_____

_____

_____

_____

_____

_____

_____

Don't wait for people to be friendly, show them how

DECEMBER 25

Don't rush things.
Anything worth
having is worth
waiting for

DECEMBER 26

Accountability

Who is in your circle? Accountability eliminates the time and effort you spend on distracting activities and other unproductive behavior.

_____
_____
_____
_____
_____
_____
_____
_____
_____
_____
_____
_____
_____
_____

DECEMBER 27

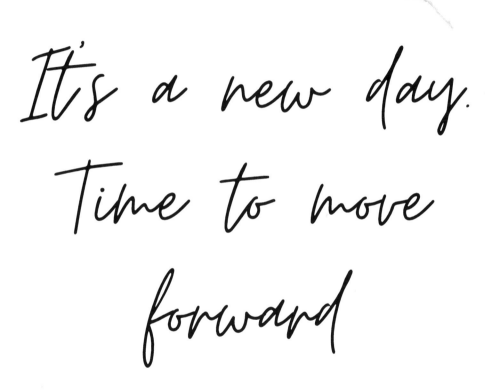

It's a new day.
Time to move
forward

You were put on this earth to achieve greatness

DECEMBER 29

Heart Check

Who do you need to forgive? Forgiveness is not for
the other person. It is for you!

_____
_____
_____
_____
_____
_____
_____
_____
_____
_____
_____
_____
_____
_____
_____
_____

Every new day is another chance to change your life

One DAE can change everything

Author Directory

A

Adams, Theresa Faith - destineetheangel3@yahoo.com

Armstead, Charla charla_armstead@yahoo.com

B

Bacon, Chanda - chandabacon@ymail.com

Banks, Mary - mbanks1527@yahoo.com

Banks, Stephanie - snelliott87@gmail.com

Bell, Lasaraha - lavivvirginhair@gmail.com

Belton, Althea - goodandfaithful1@gmail.com

Benefield, Cureene - spaghetti96@hotmail.com

Blackman, Kimberly - byfaithkb8@hotmail.com

Brookins, Dr. Sonja - sonjabrookins@gmail.com

Bryant, Cheryl - cherylbryant35@comcast.net

Bryant, Latrice - latrice_bryant@yahoo.com

Buckner, Patricia - pbuckner59@sbcglobal.net

Bunn, Inetta - inettasb@gmail.com

C

Chamberlain, Katrina - katrinahowell41@icloud.com

Charley, Lashica - charleylashica@gmail.com

Chatman, Edith - edith.chatman@yahoo.com

Chavis, Toni - chavislm@gmail.com

Church, Janie - janiechurch@focusdrivencoaching.com

D

Dallas, Chiquita - chickie0930@gmail.com

Davis, Dr, Shandra - drshandrad@gmail.com

Dunn, Rubye - imaginemellctampa@gmail.com

E

Ellington, Jennifer - womanonpurpose37@gmail.com

F

Floyd-Reynolds, Windi - focusedink@gmail.com

Foster, Leslie -lezmartinez3000@gmail.com

G

Giles, Catrena - cgiles@mail.usf.edu

Gonzalez, Nancy - mustardseedbagsofcourage@yahoo.com

Graves, Sharon - sharon.graves@ymail.com

Green, Sheila - sdgreen0808@yahoo.com

Greene, Trinnette - tringreene@yahoo.com

H

Haughton, Latarsha - latarshahaughton@gmail.com

Hebb, Ebony - thebigtheboldandbeautiful@gmail.com

H

Hills, Carla - carla.hills573@gmail.com

Hogan, LaQuita - laquita.hogan37@gmail.com

Hunter, Nitisha - nitishahunter@yahoo.com

I

Isaac, Marguerite - marguerite.isaac@gmail.com

J

Jackson, Andrea - abivens2001@hotmail.com

Jackson, Kimberland - kimberland@kimberlandjackson.com

Jackson, T'Edra - tedra@kingsskid.com

James, Dorixa - djames013@icloud.com

Jarrell, Angel - angel7jarrell@yahoo.com

Johnson, Princess - p.smith030411@gmail.com

Johnson, Robbin - robbinj7@yahoo.com

Johnson, LaTambria - latambriasmith@gmail.com

Johnson, Dr. Tylisha - tylishanjohnson@gmail.com

K

kelly, Fonda - kfaith2010@gmail.com

King, Angelette Verdena - angelette.verdena@icloud.com

Kinnel, Angela - a_kinnel@yahoo.com

L

LaGuerre, Angelica - laguerreangel@gmail.com

Legions, Vicki - aestheticsbyvicki@gmail.com

Lewis - Hairston, Shenay - Shenaylewis@gmail.com

M

McKnight, Latasha - churchlatasha@yahoo.com

McLamb, April - underthebroomtreellc@gmail.com

Moore, Markeeva - markeevalynn7@yahoo.com

N

Newby, Dr. Synetheia - snn@iamdrnewby.com

P

Pettigrew, Dorothy - dqpettigrew@gmail.com

Phillips, Andrea - andreaphillipsmft@gmail.com

Pierre, Shawntrel - shawntrelp@gmail.com

Prophete, Nahomie - nprophete1161@gmail.com

R

Ragland, Natalie - completeyourcalling@gmail.com

Robinson, Dr. Xaviera - xmcqueen@yahoo.com

Ross, Devin - devdross@gmail.com

S

Sneed-Scott, Sonya - sonyascott321@gmail.com

S

Shannon, Katera - drivenbygraceministries@yahoo.com

Shannon, Lakisha - kishajev@msn.com

Shepherd, Lorrie - projecttakeback16@gmail.com

Simmons, Sh'nai - Drshnai@Insidereachministries.org

Sinclair, Kimberly - ksinclair365@gmail.com

Smith, Kathy - kathy.smith@chandeliersforchrist.com

Smith, Cashina - cashinasmith@yahoo.com

Staples, Candace - candacestaples20@gmail.com

T

Taylor, Dorothea - theades@att.net

Thompson, Tanya - gloryaftertherain@gmail.co

Thornton, Chrissy - chrissyt75@gmail.com

Tippins, LaTisha - latisha.tippins@gmail.com

Tredway, Dani - kelleytredway@gmail.com

W

Waters, Venetia - pastorvenetia@gmail.com

Watkins, Paula - loveyourself2lifeinc@hotmail.com

Williams, Monica - mcwjc@bellsouth.net

Williams, Tarissa -tarissawilliams@gmail.com

Williams, Mikesha - mikeshalwilliams@gmail.com

Williams, Jovoni - jovoni.dawson@gmail.com

Wilson, Meoshia - meoshia.wilson@hotmail.com

Witherspoon, Shaynne - mzspoon@att.net

Made in the USA
Columbia, SC
15 May 2021

37996165R00213